# Ancient Echoes:
## the early history of a Welsh peninsula

by Julian Heath

First published in 2006

© Text: Julian Heath
© Photographs: author/Amgueddfa ac Oriel Gwynedd, Bangor

ISBN: 1-84527-093-2

Published by
Gwasg Carreg Gwalch,
12 Iard yr Orsaf, Llanrwst, Wales, LL26 0EH.
☎ 01492 642031   Fax: 01492 641502
e-mail: llyfrau@carreg-gwalch.com
www.carreg-gwalch.com

Printed and published in Wales.

*For Mum and Dad and last but not least, Margaret.*

## Acknowledgements

I would like to express my thanks to Nina Steele of Gwynedd
Archaeological Trust who answered my many queries about
ancient sites and monuments in the peninsula. I would also
like to thank Esther Roberts of Gwynedd Museum and Art
Gallery, Bangor, for supplying photographs of artefacts from
the peninsula and elsewhere in Wales. Finally, I would like to
thank Myrddin ap Dafydd for commissioning the book and
giving me the chance to write about this special place.

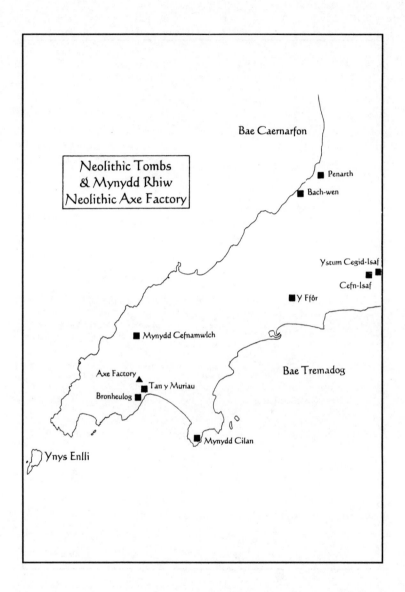

Neolithic Tombs
& Mynydd Rhiw
Neolithic Axe Factory

Bae Caernarfon

Penarth

Bach-wen

Ystum Cegid-Isaf

Cefn-Isaf

Y Ffôr

Mynydd Cefnamwlch

Axe Factory

Tan y Muriau

Bronheulog

Bae Tremadog

Mynydd Cilan

Ynys Enlli

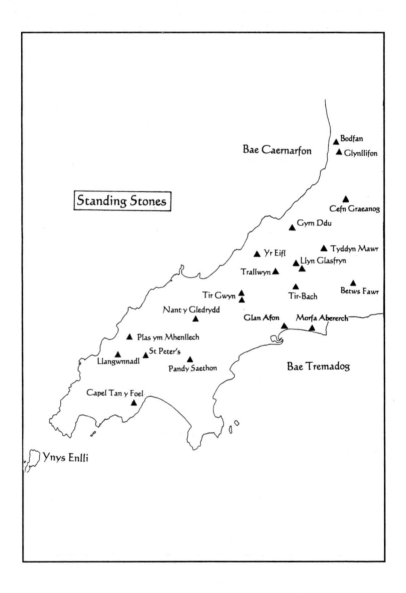

Bae Caernarfon

▲ Bodfan
▲ Glynllifon

Standing Stones

▲ Cefn Graeanog

▲ Gyrn Ddu

▲ Yr Eifl    ▲ Tyddyn Mawr
▲ Llyn Glasfryn
Trallwyn ▲

▲ Betws Fawr

Tir Gwyn ▲    ▲ Tir-Bach
▲

Nant y Gledrydd ▲    Glan Afon    Morfa Abererch
▲

▲ Plas ym Mhenllech    ▲ St Peter's
Llangwnnadl ▲    Pandy Saethon    Bae Tremadog

Capel Tan y Foel ▲

Ynys Enlli

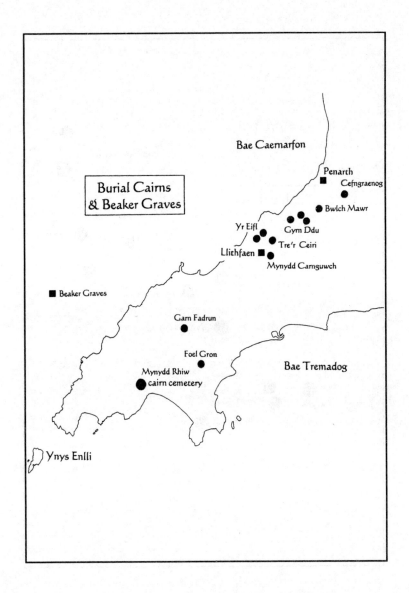

Burial Cairns
& Beaker Graves

Bae Caernarfon

Penarth
Cefngraenog
Bwlch Mawr
Yr Eifl
Gyrn Ddu
Tre'r Ceiri
Llithfaen
Mynydd Carnguwch

■ Beaker Graves

Garn Fadrun

Foel Gron
Mynydd Rhiw
cairn cemetery

Bae Tremadog

Ynys Enlli

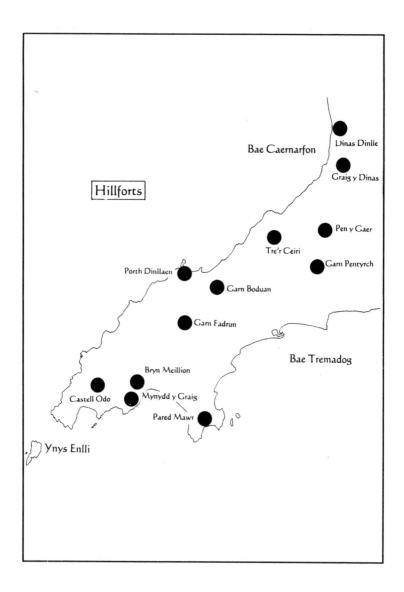

Hillforts

Bae Caernarfon

Dinas Dinlle

Graig y Dinas

Pen y Gaer

Tre'r Ceiri

Garn Pentyrch

Porth Dinllaen

Garn Boduan

Garn Fadrun

Bae Tremadog

Bryn Meillion

Castell Odo

Mynydd y Graig

Pared Mawr

Ynys Enlli

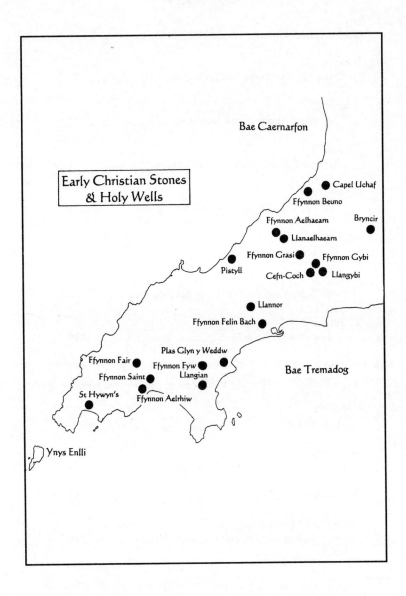

Early Christian Stones & Holy Wells

Bae Caernarfon

Capel Uchaf

Ffynnon Beuno

Ffynnon Aelhaearn

Bryncir

Llanaelhaearn

Ffynnon Grasi

Ffynnon Gybi

Pistyll

Cefn-Coch

Llangybi

Llannor

Ffynnon Felin Bach

Plas Glyn y Weddw

Ffynnon Fair

Ffynnon Fyw

Ffynnon Saint

Llangian

St Hywyn's

Ffynnon Aelrhiw

Bae Tremadog

Ynys Enlli

# Contents

# Introduction

This book is concerned with the ancient communities who lived in what are now the three cantrefi of Llŷn, Arfon and Eifionydd in Gwynedd, north-western Wales. It should perhaps be pointed out here that Eifionydd was originally a cymyd (the singular of cymydau, which are smaller divisions of the cantrefi), that along with Ardudwy, formed the cantref of Dunoding. Today however, it is largely viewed in much the same way as the cantrefi of Llŷn and Arfon and stands alone as such.

In Welsh, cantref literally means 'a hundred townships' (which were established in the early Medieval period) and as Michael Senior has pointed out in *Portrait of North Wales* it is difficult to see how a hundred villages could have ever existed in the rural cantrefi. However, this is perhaps irrelevant because as Michael Senior further notes that, for a native of Wales, "a cantref marks a distinction in one's view of life, an almost tribal territorial relationship". I do not think it would be stretching credulity too far to suggest that these relationships probably have a long heritage that stretches back into the prehistoric period.

Llŷn, Arfon and Eifionydd are situated in the long and narrow peninsula (which is often wrongly referred to as the *Lleyn Peninsula*) which juts out south-westwards into the Irish Sea, from the western edge of the Snowdonia National Park. The peninsula measures some thirty-four miles in length, from its start around Bontnewydd to its end at Ynys Enlli (*Bardsey Island*) and is around twelve miles at its widest point (from Porth Dinllaen to Mynydd Cilan).

The ancient communities who lived in this area may have long since faded into the past, but among its lonely uplands and quiet green fields they have left behind fascinating reminders of their existence. In this rugged and gentle peninsula, which possesses a unique Welsh beauty, there are numerous and diverse archaeological remains, which bear witness to the ancient people who lived here and provide a faint but compelling echo of their lives. Although many of the peninsula's ancient sites and monuments are included in the following pages, it is beyond the scope of this book to include them all. I have though, provided some useful contacts at the end of the Gazetteer for those people who would like to look even further into the peninsula's ancient history and perhaps also, more recent historical periods. This book will therefore serve as an introduction to these ancient remains and hopefully inspire people to explore for themselves the many places in Llŷn, Arfon and Eifionydd where the past still lingers.

With this purpose in mind, I have supplied a gazetteer at the end of the book which gives grid references for the main sites mentioned in the text. This can be used in conjunction with the standard Ordnance Survey map of our area of interest *(Lleyn Peninsula Landranger 123)*. As an additional aid, I have also supplied directions to the various sites featured in the book. Although many of the sites and monuments featured in the book are very easy to find, past experience has taught me that even with the aid of a map, some can be more difficult to locate! It should also be borne in mind that some of the archaeological remains mentioned in the book are situated on private land and permission should therefore be sought when visiting such places.

The book then, is first and foremost a guide to the peninsula's remarkable and fascinating ancient history but it also aims to look at this history in a broader context so that it can be better understood. Therefore, with this purpose in mind, archaeological evidence from other parts of Britain and Europe will also be discussed in the course of the book, along with some found closer to home, elsewhere in Wales. Also, those readers who decide to visit the sites and monuments mentioned in this book will also realise that many are situated in what have to be some of the most stunning landscapes in the British Isles, which I hope will provide a further incentive to visit them. For me, this has been an added bonus to writing this book and has helped to make it a hugely enjoyable experience.

The history of the peninsula begins in the Mesolithic period (c. 10000-4200 BC) and although we have no evidence for human activity earlier than this in the peninsula, there must have been people living here before this time – though they would have been few in number. It should also be pointed out that the peninsula with which we are familiar today, would not have actually formed until around 7000 BC, which unfortunately means that many Mesolithic sites have probably been lost to rising sea levels.

Our evidence for the Mesolithic period in the peninsula consists of scatters of stone tools found at various sites (e.g. Brynrefail farm near Abersoch, St Mary's church, Aberdaron and Ynys Enlli). Such tools would have been used for various tasks such as gathering wild plant foods and butchering and skinning animals. Mention should also be made here of the recent discovery of an important Mesolithic site discovered on Ynys Enlli and a team led by Mark Edmonds has been investigating this further evidence for hunter-gatherers in the peninsula.

Unfortunately, stone tools are often the only evidence we have of Mesolithic people because as hunter-gatherers they would have lived a transitory lifestyle, moving from place to place as they sought out new food sources in the wild. Therefore their settlements were not built with permanence in mind and so, have often been destroyed by later activity. Nevertheless there have been some significant finds relating to Mesolithic settlement and activity elsewhere in the British Isles, such as the seasonal hunting camps discovered at Starr Carr in Yorkshire and Mount Sandel in County Antrim.

This study therefore begins in the succeeding Neolithic period when farming first appeared in the peninsula and the people of this time left behind clear and striking evidence of their existence. We will look at the impressive and intriguing stone tombs built by the area's first farmers and also at a 'factory' were stone axes and other tools were produced by Neolithic people for use in the peninsula and elsewhere.

From here, the religious monuments left behind by the people of the early Bronze Age will be examined. These take the form of burial cairns and standing stones – the latter being perhaps the most puzzling of all prehistoric monuments.

After this, we will look at one of the most fascinating and controversial prehistoric societies of Europe – the 'Beaker

People', who may have some connection with the early Bronze Age monuments of the peninsula.

Next, the Iron Age will be considered. This seems to have been a time when tribal warfare was prevalent and the splendid hillforts of the peninsula will be examined. One of these hillforts – Tre'r Ceiri, is one of the finest examples of its kind in the British Isles, or indeed in Europe.

Finally, we are into the time of the Celtic saints and the arrival of Christianity in the peninsula. It is clear that this area played an important part in the formative years of Christianity in the British Isles and the fine archaeological evidence from the peninsula that attests to this will be discussed.

In this book then, we will go on a journey lasting some five thousand years. Along the way, we will encounter the legacy of the ancient communities who occupied this part of the British Isles and hopefully gain some understanding of their lives. More importantly, we will discover the ancient heritage of this northern Welsh peninsula, which forms an integral part in the long and remarkable history of the British Isles.

## Chapter 1

# Introduction to the Neolithic

The Neolithic period is one of the most significant chapters in the story of human development. During this time, the hunting and gathering way of life that had lasted for many millennia was replaced by one based on a farming economy. Thus the semi-nomadic groups, who had wandered the landscape living off its wild resources, began to settle down in permanent settlements whose subsistence was based on domesticated crops and animals. The significance of this change in the way human communities lived cannot be underestimated, for it shaped the course of history and ultimately, it could be said that the foundations of modern civilisation were laid during the Neolithic period.

It is now known that the Neolithic began in the Near East around 8000 BC. Gradually this way of life spread across the continent, arriving in the British Isles c. 4200 BC and ending around 2500 BC with the arrival of metalworking and the beginning of the Bronze Age. The traditional view of the arrival of the Neolithic in Europe was that its slow spread across the continent could be attributed to groups of agricultural colonists, who displaced the old hunter-gatherer lifestyle of the Mesolithic natives. It is now recognised that this view is too simplistic and that the emergence of the Neolithic in Europe was a more complicated process than originally envisaged.

What does seem highly likely, is that around 6000 BC, early farming groups who belonged to the 'Linear Pottery Culture' (so called because of their distinctive, decorated pottery) migrated from the Balkan region into the Danube Valley and settled on the fertile, loess (a fertile soil) plains of central Europe. The Linear Pottery Culture is more commonly known by the acronym LBK – after the German word for linear pottery – Linienbandkeramik. The LBK lived in villages comprising of large timber longhouses, kept livestock, grew crops and used novel items of material culture such as pottery (though pottery is known from the late Mesolithic period in Scandinavia). The remains of these settlements are rare and often insubstantial, but traces of them can still be found at places such as the Aldenhoven plateau in Germany. It seems that LBK colonists also travelled further north and west into the margins of the loess lands, settling in Holland, France and Belgium. The fortified nature of some of the sites in Belgium (e.g. Darion and Oleye in the Geer Valley) suggests that violent conflict could sometimes erupt between these early, immigrant farmers and their indigenous, Mesolithic neighbours.

It also likely that there was further movement of early farming groups from the Balkans and Greece into southern Italy. These immigrants were also marked out by their distinctive pottery vessels which were decorated using cardium (cockle) shells and thus such pottery is known as 'Cardial Impressed Ware'. After these early Neolithic communities became established in southern Italy, agriculture appears to have spread into other parts of the Mediterranean such as Sicily, southern France, and southern Portugal. This further spread of agriculture into the central and west Mediterranean may well have been initiated by sea borne colonists.

Around the areas settled by the immigrant farmers however, the situation appears to be more complex with different sets of interactions taking place between the old and new cultures of Mesolithic and Neolithic Europe. The British Isles was one of these areas and traditionally the view has been that agricultural colonists arrived here from the continent and introduced their distinctive and novel way of life. As a result, the Mesolithic natives (who were believed to be few in number) were forced to marginal areas of land where they slowly dwindled, or were assimilated into the new way of life and 'became' Neolithic.

In recent years, the more predominant view has been that the Mesolithic communities of the British Isles 'adopted' the Neolithic way of life because of contacts between themselves and Neolithic groups on the continent. There is evidence that lends support to both sides of the argument, but it seems more likely that were was some initial immigration by continental farming groups combined with native responses to the lifestyle and values of the incoming Neolithic. This may seem like a case of 'archaeological fence-sitting', but as Francis Pryor says in his excellent Britain BC: "I suspect that we will soon arrive at some form of consensus which will acknowledge the contribution made by communities on both sides of the channel".

The arrival of the Neolithic in the British Isles is a contentious issue amongst prehistorians, but although it will be touched upon we should not be too overly concerned with it. The purpose of the succeeding chapters on the Neolithic period in Llŷn, Arfon and Eifionydd is to examine the impressive and intriguing evidence left behind by the Neolithic communities of the peninsula to see what it may reveal about society at this time. Before this evidence is examined, it will be worthwhile to take a brief look at the environment and nature of life here during the Neolithic.

With its warm summers and mild winters, the climate of the present day peninsula makes life easier for its inhabitants. Their Neolithic ancestors would have lived in a similar climate, though it would have been a little warmer and wetter during this time. However, life for these early farming communities would have been hard, with high mortality rates among children and a short life span amongst adults; those people who lived into their forties would have been very old for the standards of their time. Is is also clear from studies of skeletal material that the lives of Neolithic people were blighted by osteoarthritis. This degenerative and painful condition affected the hips, the knees, the lower spine and finger-ends. It became common in the Neolithic because of the greater stresses placed on the body by the farming lifestyle (e.g. chopping down and moving trees and ploughing by hand).

Perhaps not surprisingly, Neolithic life in the British Isles did not always consist of peaceful farming communities living harmoniously with nature and each other, as archaeology has also revealed that violence and conflict were not uncommon during this time. For instance, during the excavation of an Iron Age settlement at Fengate near Peterborough a Neolithic grave containing four bodies (a male, female, infant and one individual of indeterminate sex) was discovered and a leaf-shaped arrowhead was found between the ribs of the male skeleton.

Similar evidence of violence is also known at a number of Neolithic tombs in Britain. For example at the long barrow of Ascott-under-Wychwood (Oxfordshire), a male skeleton in the southern-most burial chamber had a leaf-shaped arrowhead beneath a rib, while at a chambered cairn near Loch Calder, Caithness a broken, flint arrowhead was found embedded in the lower vertebra of an adult male. Other evidence of Neolithic violence could be cited and one wonders how many of the arrowheads commonly assumed to be grave goods represent the weapons that actually killed people?

How these people died is unclear, but it is possible that they met their end in large-scale Neolithic conflicts, for which there is strong evidence in southern Britain. At the well-known Neolithic, 'causewayed enclosure' at Crickley Hill on the Cotswold scarp, excavations revealed that the fortified settlement had been attacked at least twice and hundreds of arrowheads were found concentrated around the gateways and the line of the former palisade. Hambledon Hill in Dorset also features the remains of a fortified causewayed enclosure that was attacked and set on fire. Two male skeletons were discovered under the remains of the collapsed rampart (probably a result of the fire) and leaf-shaped arrowheads had killed both. One of the skeletons (a young male aged about 19) provided a particularly poignant reminder, that as in the conflicts of our time, the innocent also suffered in those of the Neolithic. Underneath the chest of the young man, the remains of a child were also found and it appears that he was trying to save it from the attack on the enclosure when he was struck in the chest by an arrow.

Causewayed enclosures are found in many parts of north-western and central Europe and while the evidence found at Crickley and Hambledon Hill reveals that they were used as fortified refuges, it is clear that this was not their only function and archaeologists have struggled to understand these mysterious monuments. The layouts of causewayed enclosures are very varied, but a 'typical' example consists of one or more circuits of short ditches and banks that are interrupted by undug gaps or 'causeways' of earth or chalk, which give access into the enclosure (from the air the ditches look rather like strings of sausages!). The fact that these earthwork boundaries are discontinuous lessens their effectiveness as defensive places, as there would be many weak points in the circuits. Therefore many causewayed enclosures were probably not designed primarily with defence in mind, though some sites do seem to have been definitely fortified.

Many archaeologists have therefore interpreted most causewayed enclosures as meeting places where rituals and ceremonies of a religious and secular nature took place. Archaeological evidence found in the ditches of causewayed enclosures seems to confirm this, with their ditches filled with such things as animal bones from feasts, broken pottery, complete axes and chalk 'cult' objects. Human bones are also often found in ditches and at Hambledon Hill for example, human skulls were deliberately placed along the bottom of the ditch, suggesting some type of ritual activity. However, these skulls have been interpreted as possible evidence of 'head-hunting' by Neolithic warriors, which has been documented among a number of 'primitive' societies around the world. Archaeological and literary evidence also reveals that there was a cult of the human head in Iron Age Europe (the head was seen as the seat of the soul) and that the warriors of this time almost certainly practiced head-hunting. It is quite possible therefore, that their Neolithic ancestors held similar beliefs and likewise, undertook head-hunting missions in which they sought to 'capture' enemy souls.

Equally as enigmatic as the causewayed enclosures – if not more so – are the Neolithic 'cursus' monuments which seem to be confined to the British Isles. They appear to date from c. 3700-2900 BC and consist of two parallel ditches with the upcast from the ditches normally forming two parallel inner banks (though sometimes this ditch material was used to form a long mound that ran down the central space). Often the ends of the cursus are closed off, but they could be left open. There is great variation in their length, with some cursuses only reaching about 150m, while others travel for miles across the landscape (e.g. the Dorset Cursus is over six miles long). They are very puzzling monuments, but their alignment on other Neolithic monuments such as long barrows and henges (the Dorset cursus for example, had two long barrows positioned at either end of it) suggests that they were used as processional ways in religious rituals and ceremonies. It is also likely that a number of curseses were aligned on astronomical events and for example, one end of the Dorset cursus was oriented towards the midwinter sunset.

Henges and stone circles are the other main classes of monument that were built during the later stages of the Neolithic and again it would be fair to assume, on the basis of the evidence found at them, that they were places connected with rituals and ceremonies. There are over six hundred stone circles still surviving in the British Isles and their form and size varies greatly. Some stone circles measure only 10 metres in diameter, while others have a diameter measuring over 110 metres (e.g. Long Meg and Her Daughters, Cumbria). It is also evident that many stone circles were erected in order to observe the movements of the sun and the moon and it seems highly likely that such orientations are connected with prehistoric religious ideas and practices.

Henges are circular earthworks that feature an inner ditch surrounded by an outer bank, with two opposing entrances (or sometimes one) leading into the interior space. Like the stone circles they vary greatly in size and some massive examples still survive on the Wessex chalklands. These henges range in size from 320-480 metres (which has led to them being called 'super henges') and even today some five thousand years later, the ditch at the Avebury henge monument in Wiltshire has to be seen to be believed. The most famous henge is of course Stonehenge, but this is an atypical example as the henge found here has the bank encircling the ditch on the inside rather than the outside.

Turning now to the more mundane aspects of Neolithic life, we will take a brief look at one of the defining characteristics of the Neolithic – pottery. As in many places in Europe, pottery was not known in the British Isles in the preceding Mesolithic period and must have been introduced into these islands from the continent. The fact that the earliest Neolithic pottery (known as Grimston ware after a site in Yorkshire) displays skill and sophistication in its manufacture, lends support to the view that it was immigrant farming groups who were responsible for the inception of the Neolithic in the British Isles. Similar pottery is known from sites in Wales (e.g. Llandegai) and is known as 'Irish Sea Ware'.

As the Neolithic became established, new forms of pottery were made and regional styles appeared. For example, in Scotland we have Unstan and Beachara wares, while in central and eastern England we find Mildenhall and Abdingdon wares. Pottery resembling Abingdon ware is found on Welsh sites such as the Neolithic long cairns of Ty Isaf and Tinkinswood in Southern Wales

In the later Neolithic a distinctive form of pottery known as 'Grooved ware' came into use and it is clear that these highly decorated vessels have an affinity with megalithic art found in Neolithic passage graves. Until recently, Grooved Ware had not been confirmed in Wales, but we now have finds from places such as Trelystan (Powys) and Lligwy tomb on Anglesey.

Pollen records gathered by archaeologists from prehistoric contexts reveal that much of the British Isles would have been covered in deciduous woodland. Even upland areas of Britain such as Dartmoor were covered in forests and. pollen studies from Wales suggest that the peninsula would have been covered in extensive alder woodland, with subsidiary oak and birch woods. In particular, the sheltered valleys must have been clothed in dense woodland – providing a serious challenge for the stone axes of the early farmers. It was during the Neolithic that this woodland began to be cleared and the patchwork of fields and farms that can be seen today in the peninsula ultimately have their origins in these early tree clearances.

The dense woodlands of the Early Neolithic peninsula would have been cleared using sharp stone axes and there have been stray finds of stone axes at places such as Bryn

Marsli, Chwilog and Uwch Mynydd. Of greater importance however, is the Neolithic axe 'factory' situated on the windy headland of Mynydd Rhiw. Stone axes made at this site travelled far from their original source and have been found at places such as Pen Dinas, Aberystwyth and Craswall Priory in Herefordshire. These finds provide evidence of Neolithic 'trade' in the peninsula and this issue will be discussed further when we to turn to look at the Mynydd Rhiw axe factory in more detail in Chapter 3.

Along with other woodworking activities, stone axes would also have been used for the construction of timber dwellings in which the Neolithic people of the peninsula would have lived. What these dwellings looked like is unknown, because as yet, no Neolithic house has been found here. However, we do have examples of such houses from elsewhere in Wales and the British Isles, which indicate the probable form that the Neolithic houses of the peninsula took.

The best known Neolithic houses come from famous prehistoric settlement of Skara Brae on Orkney, which was occupied during the late Neolithic (c.3100 –2450 BC) and the well-preserved stone houses found here provide a remarkable insight into Neolithic life. However, the Neolithic stone houses of Skara Brae seem to be unique to this area and it is unlikely (but not impossible) that similar settlements existed in other parts of the British Isles.

In general, excavated examples of the houses in which the first farmers lived are rare in the British Isles, though around a hundred are known in Ireland and some good example of Neolithic houses have also been found in Wales. The Neolithic house found at Ballynagilly in Ireland is around 6000 years old and as such, is the earliest example of a Neolithic house in Britain or Ireland. Houses in the earlier Neolithic were mainly square or rectangular in shape, while those from the later Neolithic tended to be round or oval – revealing a change in architectural style. It is evident that many Neolithic domestic structures were modest in scale and made from timber, as revealed by postholes, stakeholes and rare bedding trenches for posts. Inside they seem to have mainly consisted of a single living space, though houses could be divided internally by walls and the remains of simple hearths have also been found at some sites. It should perhaps also be pointed out here, that some Neolithic 'houses' may have actually been structures connected with Neolithic religious and ceremonial practices rather than domestic buildings.

One of the finest examples of a Neolithic house in Wales was discovered at Llandygái near Bangor and here, the remains of an earlier Neolithic house were found under a later Neolithic henge monument. Although evidence of occupation within the house was missing, deep postholes were discovered. These revealed that a rectangular, wooden building 13 metres long and 6 metres wide had once stood on the site and that it had been divided internally into three separate areas.

The largest Neolithic settlement to have survived in Wales is found on the hilltop of Clegyr Boia near St David's in Pembrokeshire. Here, there had been at least three Neolithic houses, though the plan of the building found in the 1920's is unclear. House 1 seems to have comprised of a rectangular building measuring 7 by 4 metres, which was covered by a ridged roof. External cooking areas were found outside the house along with a midden where domestic refuse was dumped. House 2 which had been burnt down at some point appears to have been a similar but smaller building than House 1.

Actual evidence for the crops and animals that where present on Neolithic farms in Wales is scarce but nevertheless, emmer wheat, barley, celtic beans, cattle, pig, sheep and goats are known to have been present. It is also evident that wild plant foods such as blackberries, crab apples and hazelnuts were gathered and that hunting and fishing must have further supplemented the diets of the first farmers, though in general there is a curious lack of evidence of this.

It is also worth mentioning here, an extraordinary find from the causewayed enclosure at Hambledon Hill, which was mentioned above in light of Neolithic warfare. The find was extremely small (5mm long) and was a carbonised grape pip, which had been preserved by chance in the fire that swept through the settlement. This fortuitous find could represent the import of exotic, dried fruit from the continent or perhaps it is even possible that the Neolithic people of Wessex were growing grapes?

The general lack of evidence for substantial Neolithic farms, which suggest a settled agricultural lifestyle, is now largely taken as implying that many of the first farmers in the British Isles led a nomadic lifestyle and that they were practising a type of 'swidden cultivation'. This form of agriculture is known among many tribal peoples and involves the clearing of forest for short-term cultivation of crops and a greater emphasis on pastoralism (the regular movement of animals between seasonal grazing areas), with settlements lasting no more than a couple of years. However, we should also bear in mind that later agricultural and building activity may have destroyed much of the evidence that once existed for Neolithic settlements of a more permanent nature.

To prepare ground for cultivation, Neolithic people used a simple type of hand-drawn plough known as an 'ard' and ard-marks have been found beneath the South Street long barrow near Avebury. A 'rip-ard' (a sturdier ard that had a deeper point for digging) had been used to plough the soil and it had reached so deep that it left marks on the chalk bedrock. Rip-ards were substantial pieces of equipment and teams of oxen must have drawn them.

It may well be, as many archaeologists now believe, that the Mesolithic natives of the British Isles played a significant part in the appearance of farming in these islands. While this does seem likely, studies of ancient DNA provide evidence that there must have been some migration by continental farming groups into the British Isles. These studies by Brian Sykes of Oxford University revealed that nearly all of the population of Europe is descended from seven females who had lived between c. 43000-8000 BC. Syke's analysis also revealed that one of these women (Jasmine) was born in Syria around ten thousand years ago. Syria forms part of the 'Fertile Crescent' where domesticated crops and animals first appeared around 8000 BC. Syke's studies further revealed that 17% of Jasmine's descendants are found along routes that are traditionally associated with the spread of the first farmers in Europe, which has been discussed above. The first of these routes runs north-west across Central Europe towards the Channel, while the other runs from the northern Mediterranean and heads up the Rhone Valley and across France to the British Isles.

Unfortunately however, the true identity of the people who made up the Neolithic farming communities of the peninsula is hidden in the past. They may have been Mesolithic natives who had adopted the Neolithic 'package' from their neighbours. Alternatively, the first farming communities in the peninsula may have comprised of a mixture of natives and newcomers and it is this scenario that is perhaps the most probable. These newcomers may have travelled up the Irish Sea (or over it), perhaps from the West Country or even further afield, from places such as Brittany and Iberia.

One thing is clear however; these early communities left behind them in the glorious landscape of the peninsula, hugely impressive and intriguing funerary monuments where they deposited their dead. These will be examined in the next chapter, which is concerned with the megalithic tombs of Llŷn, Arfon and Eifionydd.

## Chapter 2

# Ancestral tombs of the Neolithic

One of the most enduring aspects of the Neolithic period are the large funerary monuments that were built for the disposal of the dead. At a basic level, there are two different types of funerary monuments – *megalithic tombs* with stone burial chambers and non-megalithic tombs or *earthen long barrows*, which contain wooden burial chambers. It is with the former monuments that we are concerned, as a number of these tombs still survive in the peninsula.

The megalithic tombs of the Neolithic are concentrated in countries along the Atlantic seaboard of Europe and many fine examples of these structures can still be seen in Portugal, Spain, Brittany, France and the British Isles (with some magnificent examples in Ireland, Brittany and the Orkneys). They are also found in Scandinavia, Holland and north Germany. The architecture of the megalithic tombs varies greatly, but the archaeological evidence indicates a common theme of collective burial.

It is evident that jumbled masses of bone belonging to both adults and children were often deposited in the burial chambers of megalithic tombs. Analysis of the skeletal remains from Neolithic burial chambers often shows that bones are bleached and weathered, which suggests that they were left outside for some time before being deposited in the tombs. It is highly likely that this evidence reveals that Neolithic people left the bodies of the deceased to decompose, before they were placed in the burial chambers of tombs. It is also quite possible that in some cases, this 'defleshing' process took place on timber scaffolds, which were erected for this purpose. At the Neolithic tomb of Isbister on Orkney, the bleached and weathered bones found here showed no signs of carnivore's teeth marks and this led the excavator of the cairn to make the plausible suggestion that the bodies may therefore been set up on such a scaffold. Such 'defleshing scaffolds' have been recorded among native

24

tribes of North America, such as the Dakota and Choctaw. The exact thinking behind the practice of defleshing will remain with the people of this time, but it is likely to be related to the idea that the soul can only be set free from the body after its flesh has rotted away. This is a belief that has been documented in many 'primitive' societies of a more recent date. For example, the Hopewell Indians in Ohio only buried their dead after the flesh had rotted, or been sliced from their corpses, so that the sprits of the dead could journey to the other-world. The Tibetans and Zoroastrians of ancient Persia believed that defleshing the body allowed the spirit to reunite with the four elements of air, earth, fire and water. As with the Hopewell Indians, we also have examples of flesh being sliced from the bones in Neolithic contexts in Belgium. In the Trou du Frontal near Furfooz, a collective burial was discovered in a rock-fissure and about 50 of the bones showed clear cut-marks where the flesh had been cut off with sharp flint tools. However, it should be pointed out here, that this evidence could be related to acts of ritual cannibalism, which in some cases may been carried out by victorious warriors on enemies they had defeated in battle. An example of this can probably be seen at the Late Mesolithic site of Dyrholmen in Denmark. Here, human long bones had been split so that their marrow could be reached and there was also evidence of beheading and scalping. Similar evidence to this has been found at several prehistoric sites across Europe and may be related to the idea that by eating they flesh of your enemy you were absorbing the power of his soul.

It should also be mentioned that in some areas during the Neolithic, cremation was the dominant funerary rite in tombs, though similar beliefs regarding the departure of the soul to the otherworld probably still existed in these areas. The Neolithic people, who practised cremation, probably felt that the burning of the body released a person's spirit from its earthly host.

In regard to the megalithic tombs, the noted prehistorian Frances Lynch has rightly said that they "can still inspire awe, wonder and curiosity in modern populations familiar with Gothic cathedrals and towering skyscrapers".

Thousands of years after their construction, megalithic tombs still stand as a testament to the engineering skills of people who had only the most basic of tools. They also offer us a tantalising glimpse into the shadowy but intriguing world of Neolithic religion.

As mentioned above, several megalithic tombs can still be seen in the peninsula and they will be examined in this chapter. Their possible religious and social significance in light of Neolithic society will also be discussed and our visit to these fascinating monuments will begin with the class of tombs known as *portal dolmens.*

**Portal Dolmens**
The archaeological evidence strongly suggests that this type of megalithic tomb dates to the early Neolithic, in the centuries around 4000 BC. They are common not only in many parts of Wales, but also in Ireland and Cornwall and, those of Wales and Ireland are very similar in design. It is hard to say for sure what this shared religious practice reveals, though it is possible that Neolithic farming groups from the continent, who had the same cultural traditions, made their way up the Atlantic coast and settled in both Wales and Ireland. On the other hand, it could be that that there was much travelling back and forth between the two countries and that the Mesolithic natives were exchanging novel religious ideas and practices. Whatever the truth is regarding the Portal Dolmens, at the very least, they indicate that Wales and Ireland shared similar religious traditions during the early Neolithic period.

Although many of the megalithic tombs of the peninsula are not 'classic' portal dolmens, they do share distinctive architectural traits associated with them and can be said to belong to the portal dolmen 'tradition'. A classic portal dolmen consists of an H-shaped arrangement of stones (the portal), which fronts a single rectangular burial chamber (in effect, a stone box) covered by a capstone, which in many cases is huge. Originally, cairns of round or rectangular stones would have covered some portal dolmens as evidenced by traces of these which still remain at some sites and it is also probable that some portal dolmens were free standing and lacking a covering mound.

Before we move on to examine the portal dolmens of the peninsula, it should be noted that archaeological excavations at Neolithic tombs in Wales have revealed a dichotomy in burial practices. The evidence indicates that cremation was favoured in the west, whilst unburned bones were deposited in the south-eastern tombs. However, although there seem to have been different funerary traditions in Wales during the Neolithic, these were still concerned with collective burial. Whether cremation was favoured in the peninsula is something we shall probably never know for certain, though it is quite probable. What we do know for certain, is that the people who lived here built imposing and intriguing monuments in which they deposited their dead. We will now begin our investigation of these monuments with the portal dolmen found near the village of Y Ffôr

### Y Ffôr (1)

This small tomb stands in a field on Cromlech (trans. From the Welsh – stone with a bent back) farm, some two miles from Pwllheli and commands fine views across Eifionydd towards Snowdonia and central Wales. As Frances Lynch points out in *Megalithic Enquiries in the West of Britain*, the ridge on which the tomb is situated provides a good route across the peninsula. This route avoids the large areas of marshy land to the east and comes out near the village of Clynnog Fawr.

The tomb that we see today represents a 1936 restoration, but it probably provides a good indication of the original appearance of the burial chamber. Interestingly, an article in *Archaeologia Cambrensis* 1877 mentions an avenue of stones (138ft in length by c. 16 feet in width) leading to the tomb. A much weathered standing stone (which now looks like a large, rounded boulder) can still be seen today in a nearby field to the north of the tomb and perhaps represents all that remains of this avenue.

### Cefn-Isaf (2)

The burial chamber at Cefn-Isaf is located in a field in the quiet village of Rhos-lan, some 2.5 miles from the village of

Llanystumdwy. It is a rather small tomb that has been partly ruined, as the stone that would have formed the south-eastern side of the chamber no longer exists. Intriguingly, it is also possible that a stone circle once surrounded the tomb, as recalled by local people in the early 20th century. Like its counterpart at Y Ffôr the tomb at Cefn-Isaf also stands near a route that provided good access across the peninsula. It is also not far from the passage grave at Ystum Cegid-Isaf, which lies about 1.5 miles to the east across the Afon Dwyfor.

### Bach Wen (3)

This tomb stands close to the sea near the village of Clynnog Fawr and its location can only be described as impressive. Behind the chamber, the peaks of Gyrn Goch and Gyrn Ddu loom large and the distinctive triple peaks of Yr Eifl can be seen to the south-west. This tomb is situated in one of the most striking and beautiful corners of the peninsula and the high peaks that rise behind the burial chamber lend it a dramatic air. It is hard to escape the feeling that the peaks of Gyrn Goch and Gyrn Ddu had some part to play in the location of this tomb.

However, leaving aside aesthetic considerations, it is the evidence left behind by Neolithic people on the capstone of the burial chamber which lends this monument its real fascination.

This evidence takes the form of about 110 artificial 'cupmarks' or small hollows that cover the upper surface of the capstone. A long curving line and a short, straight one also appear on the capstone and appear to link up some of the cupmarks. Unfortunately, the passage of time has rendered these carvings rather indistinct, but we do have an illustration of them from an article by E.L. Barnwell in *Archaeologia Cambrensis* 1867. This provides a clear picture of how the cupmarks originally appeared on the capstone. In addition to the large number of cupmarks found on the upper surface of the capstone, there are also 8 on its eastern side.

Cupmarks are found throughout the British Isles and Europe on many monuments dating to the Neolithic and the Bronze Age and are also found carved into open-air outcrops of rock. Like all 'megalithic art' cupmarks are enigmatic, prehistoric symbols but it is clear that that they had a connection to the dead as evidenced by those found on the capstone of the Bach wen tomb. A more famous example of cupmarks in association with a megalithic tomb, are those found on the fabulously decorated kerbstones that surround the magnificent Neolithic passage grave at Newgrange in Ireland. Cupmarks are also found carved into single standing stones and stones found in stone circles. An example of a single cup-marked stone was found at Plas ym Mhenllech farm in Llŷn, which now stands near the entrance into a stackyard (though the cup-marks appear to have weathered away). The original context of the stone is unknown but it is possible that it may have come from the Neolithic tomb at Mynydd Cefnamwlch (which lies about half a mile away), though this perhaps is a little unlikely. Cupmarks can also be seen on other megalithic tombs in Wales and examples include Trelyffant in Pembrokeshire and Dyffryn Ardudwy in Meirionnydd.

The true meaning of the cupmarks on the capstone of the Bach Wen tomb is lost to us, but it is conceivable that they had some 'magical' purpose and that they represent the sun or moon, or perhaps even the stars. Some support for the idea that the cupmarks on the Bach Wen tomb had an astronomical symbolism, may be provided by the cupmarks that appear on some of the huge, stone blocks that feature in the recumbent stone circles of Aberdeenshire. It is apparent that the recumbent blocks were 'aligned' by the builders of these distinctive stone circles on the midsummer full moon and pieces of white quartz found scattered in some of these circles may well have had a lunar symbolism. It is even harder to speculate about the meaning of the straight and curving lines that link some of the cupmarks, but is it possible perhaps that they represent some kind of journey? The Hopi Indians of northern Arizona drew spiral symbols, which were linked by straight lines and these represented the journey of life, with the spiral symbols representing the 'Sun Father, the giver of life.' Of course, analogies such as these may be interesting and provide us with ideas about the religious beliefs of prehistoric people, but ultimately, they cannot provide the truth.

Whatever the reality behind the cupmarks they appear to provide clear proof that as with more modern religions, symbols played an important part in the ceremonies and rituals of Neolithic and Bronze Age religion.

### Mynydd Cefnamwlch *(11)*

This is an interesting tomb and like the example at Bach Wen, it stands in an impressive location. The tomb is situated above a valley of the Afon Soch in fertile farmland near the western coast of Llŷn and as is often the case, has fine views over the surrounding countryside. Garn Fadrun with its distinctive profile is immediately apparent to the north-east and beyond this the peaks of Yr Eifl can be seen rising in the distance.

The tomb appears to belong to the portal dolmen tradition, but large stones lying near the chamber cast some doubt on this classification. The prostate stone lying close to the chamber on the west appears to be too big in relation to the rest of the tomb and that lying to the side of the chamber is rather ambiguous. It may have been a capstone that was discarded for some reason or it could represent the capstone of another chamber? Like other megalithic tombs in the peninsula, it lies near a good route that provides access inland from the coast.

### Tan y Muriau Long Cairn *(5, 6)*

This fascinating monument is perhaps the most important megalithic tomb in the peninsula. It is located on the eastern slopes of Mynydd Rhiw and consists of two chambers (originally there were three), which were set in a long cairn that was around 120ft long, traces of which, can still be seen. The long cairn faces uphill (as was often the case with tombs of this type) towards the north-west and at its northern end there is a classic portal dolmen with a massive capstone. Behind the dolmen there is a smaller side chamber which also has a capstone of no mean proportions. In 1871, J.G. Williams noted a further chamber at the southern end of the cairn and although it can no longer be observed, large stones were noted by the archaeologist, W.F. Grimes in the early

20th century. I myself have observed a large slab-like stone in the end of the cairn on my many visits to this tomb.

What we appear to have at Tan y Muriau is an isolated example of a Cotswold-Severn long cairn. There are around 130 of these monuments found mainly between Oxford and Bristol, but they are also found near Avebury in Wiltshire and there is a group found in south Wales also. The fascinating question raised by the long cairn at Tan y Muriau, is whether it represents a movement of people into Llŷn bringing new ideas about tomb building. As Frances Lynch has pointed out, a noticeable indentation of the cairn behind the portal dolmen suggests perhaps, that like a similar tomb at Dyffryn Ardudwy (Meirionnydd) the long cairn was built in two stages and may indicate the adoption of new ideas about tomb building. This question can only be answered by excavation, but at the least, Tan y Muriau long cairn indicates contact with Neolithic communities in southern Britain.

**Ystum Cegid-Isaf** *(7)*
Like its neighbour at Cefn-Isaf, this tomb is situated close to the Afon Dwyfor and the remains found here represent a type of megalithic tomb known as a passage grave. Many examples of these tombs still survive in Europe and the British Isles and they take their name from the roofed passages that led into the burial chambers. Remains of the uprights that supported the passage of Ystum Cegid-Isaf can still be observed today. It is highly probable that a round cairn originally covered the burial chamber and there is a fair chance that settlers from outside the peninsula erected this tomb. W.F. Grimes drew comparisons with the famous Bryn Celli Ddu passage grave on Anglesey and it is even possible that a group from here may have built the passage grave at Ystum Cegid-Isaf.

Passage graves, which were built in both the earlier and later Neolithic, are found in many areas of Europe and like the portal dolmens are concentrated in countries along the Atlantic seaboard, with perhaps the finest examples found in Ireland and France. At the magnificent tomb at Newgrange in Co. Meath, the passage is oriented to the south-east so that the rays of the rising sun shine down it into the burial chamber on the midwinter solstice. This deliberate orientation provides firm evidence that solar phenomena played an important part in the religious beliefs and practices of Neolithic people.

Unfortunately, the beliefs of the people who built the passage graves are lost to us but they may have been similar to those of the Batammaliba people of Togo and Benin in Africa whose shrines are built facing west, so that the rays of the setting sun fall upon them. When this occurs it is believed that the sun god is communicating with the dead elders of the tribe. Alternatively, it could be suggested that the passage grave builders aligned the passages on solar phenomena because they believed that the rays of the sun would 'reanimate' the bones of the ancestors and breathe life back into the dead. It could also be, as Alisdair Whittle has suggested, that the passages were intended for the exit of souls and spirits as well as entrances for the living.

As regards to the orientation of the passage at Ystum Cegid-Isaf, it appears that originally, it would have faced towards the north-eastern horizon, which is where the sun rises in midsummer. Unfortunately, because the passage is now destroyed, it is hard to say with any certainty whether it was deliberately aligned on this celestial event, though it remains possible that the builders of this isolated passage grave were concerned with the rays of the midsummer sun.

### Ruined Megalithic Tombs
A number of tombs still survive in the peninsula, which have for one reason or another have not stood the test of time quite as well as the others studied above. While we cannot classify them definitively, it seems probable that like many other tombs in the peninsula these ruined tombs belong to the portal dolmen tradition.

### Bronheulog (8)
The remains of this tomb consist of a large capstone and some large stones which appear to be the remains of supporting stones. It is located just behind the fine country house at Plas yn Rhiw (now owned by the National Trust

and worth a visit) in a field that commands magnificent views over Porth Neigwl. The holy well of Ffynon Aelrhiw also lies nearby and interestingly, this 'pairing' of Neolithic tombs and Holy Wells has been documented in other parts of Wales and can also be seen with the Bach Wen tomb and the well of Beuno at Clynnog Fawr. It is also worth considering the relationship between this tomb and the Tan y Muriau long cairn, which lies only about a mile to the south-west. It is likely that the latter monument is later in date, but were the two used at the same time, with each tomb belonging to different Neolithic groups on Rhiw, or did the Bronheulog tomb fall out of use with the building of Tan y Muriau long cairn?

## Penarth *(9)*

This tomb lies in quiet countryside not far from the village of Aberdesach on the peninsula's western coast in Arfon and is situated in a gently sloping field from which the peaks of Yr Eifl can be clearly seen. It is perhaps the smallest Neolithic tomb to be found in the peninsula (the Cefn-Isaf tomb is also modest in size) and now consists of a slipped capstone with three supporters. Loose boulders can also be seen lying between the supporters and these may represent the remains of the covering cairn.

## Mynydd Cilan *(10)*

This monument can be found on the headland of Penrhyn Cilan in one of the quietest and most attractive parts of the peninsula. From the tomb, there are fine views towards Porth Ceiriad beach and the headland of Trwyn yr Wylfa. The large and bulky capstone (measuring about 10.5 x 4 ft.) now lies flat in a field that slopes down to the secluded cove at Muriau, which belongs to the National Trust. Stone fragments can still be seen under the capstone, which represent the remains of supporters that have been crushed by the weight of the collapsed capstone. A photo in *Archaeologia Cambrensis* (1923) shows the capstone near a hedge and sitting at an angle on a supporting stone on it southern side. An elderly resident of the area – a Mr J. Jones – reported that another supporter was once visible on the northern side and that he had heard that there had originally been three supporting stones visible.

## The Meaning of the Megaliths

We know then, that the Neolithic people of the peninsula built large and impressive funerary monuments and that they were used for collective burial, but can these fascinating structures tell us anything more about the people who built them? This is question that has fascinated scholars and laymen alike for hundreds of years and no doubt will continue to do so. Therefore, it will be worthwhile taking a look at main issues that arise when considering this question.

### Houses for the Ancestors

It is highly probable that the earthen long barrows of the British Isles and the continent have their origin in the timber longhouses of the Linear Pottery Culture/LBK, who as we have seen, introduced farming into central and western Europe. They probably represent, as Joshua Pollard has said, 'a symbolic transformation of earlier houses' and so in essence, the houses of the living acted as the model for the houses of the dead.

How the idea of earthen long barrows first appeared in the British Isles is unclear, but is likely that Neolithic farming groups who were descended from the LBK, crossed the channel bringing with them their distinctive burial practices. In the west and the north, megalithic tombs became the dominant type of tomb, though it is unclear whether new people or new ideas account for their appearance. It should be pointed out though that megalithic tombs first appear in the Mesolithic 'heartlands' on the edges of the new farming economy – indicating some type of native response to the incoming Neolithic. Whatever the reality of their introduction into the British Isles, we have stone counterparts to the earthen long barrows, but what was the actual ideology that drove people to build such structures? It must have been powerful, as there would have been far easier ways of disposing of the dead.

The general consensus among archaeologists and

prehistorians is that there was an ancestor cult among many Neolithic societies. Ethnographic studies have shown that many 'primitive' societies, who live close to nature, worship ancestors in the belief that they watch over the well being of the community. Whilst not proving Neolithic ancestor worship, such ethnographic evidence does suggest its likelihood.

We have to bear in mind that the first farmers would have seen the natural world in a different light to us. They did not have the benefit of science to help explain the mysteries of nature; the seasons, wind, rain, storms, the fertility of crops and animals, the sun and moon. For Neolithic people natural phenomena such as these would have belonged to the world of gods and spirits. It is likely that it was left to sprits of the ancestors to intercede in this world on their behalf.

### Territorial markers

In his notable study of the megalithic tombs of Arran, Colin Renfrew argued that the modest megalithic tombs found here also acted as territorial markers of the small Neolithic communities who lived on the island. This is an attractive theory and worth considering in regard to the megalithic tombs of Llŷn, Arfon and Eifionydd.

Like the tombs on Arran, those of the peninsula are situated on or near good agricultural land and as pointed out previously, lie close to routes that must have been used by Neolithic people. A number of tombs are also in prominent locations that overlook stretches of coastline and the tombs at Mynydd Cilan, Bronheulog, Tan y Muriau and Bach Wen stand out in this respect.

Trevor Garnham has pointed out in his fine study of the Neolithic monuments of Orkney, that the Neolithic, chambered cairns found here 'were built both to be seen from and to overlook a particular area' and this statement seems to hold true for many of the peninsula's Neolithic tombs. Therefore this suggests that the tombs of the peninsula were deliberately placed in these areas and may have acted as signalling devices for people who belonged to different communities, warning them that they were in 'foreign' territory which was farmed and fished by another group. In effect, by building megalithic tombs, Neolithic communities were not only probably honouring the ancestors but may also have been using them to express their claims to the land that they owned.

The theory that megalithic tombs acted as territorial markers is a very plausible one that carries some weight and reminds us that we should not only consider the funerary role of the tombs but also the social implications of these monuments.

## Tombs for an élite?

Staying on the theme of the social implications of the megalithic tombs, we should also consider whether they reflect social differences in Neolithic society. Some archaeologists feel that the practice of collective burial in megalithic tombs indicates that Neolithic society was egalitarian in nature, with the importance of the group taking precedence over the individual.

However, many archaeologists now question this view and feel that megalithic tombs actually reflect a society that was socially differentiated and there does appear to be some evidence in support of this. For example, Aubrey Burl has pointed out that in the long barrows on Salisbury Plain, which he surmises were in use for at least a century, the average number of bodies found only amounts to six. A similar situation has been noted in the chambers of megalithic tombs and it is evident that skeletal remains found in these represent only a sample of larger Neolithic communities. Such evidence does strongly suggest that in certain areas dominant lineages or tribes came to dominate Neolithic society and that some megalithic tombs indicate the presence of such people.

Of course, it could be argued that burials were symbolic or dedicatory in nature and need not imply social ranking. It should also be noted that many of the megalithic tombs of the peninsula are modest in scale and these suggest perhaps that they were the burial places of small, scattered communities or kinship groups of the Early Neolithic who were egalitarian in nature. However, one monument – Tan-y -Muriau long cairn – suggests perhaps, that in some areas of the peninsula society was socially divided and that there were dominant groups who were in control.

As mentioned above, this monument belongs to the wider family of tombs belonging to the Cotswold-Severn group and as Joshua Pollard has pointed out these tombs 'projected an image of social difference between particular groups in society'. For example, at the famous Cotswold-Severn tomb of West Kennet in Wiltshire the burial chambers originally contained human remains that had been sorted according to age and sex. The main chamber in the innermost part of the tomb contained only males both old and young; the inner pair of facing chambers contained a mixture of male and female adults, while the outer pair held the remains of young and old people. Although it seems likely, we cannot prove that these people were among the top rank in Neolithic society but it does strongly suggest social divisions and that males dominated society.

As already mentioned Tan y Muriau long cairn originally featured three burial chambers and we have to ask ourselves why it was felt necessary to build three separate chambers? Although the people who were laid to rest in these chambers have long since gone, it is probable that here too, people were 'sorted' in death as they were in other Cotswold-Severn tombs and this also reflected social differences based on gender.

It is also possible that the people interred in the tomb belonged to a Neolithic élite who were in control in the south- western part of the peninsula and their dominance could be reflected in the tomb itself. In its original form, it would have been a huge and imposing monument and much time and effort would have gone into its construction and a monument this size must surely have required a large workforce. Somebody must have been in charge of these people and organised the construction of Tan y Muriau. The intriguing question is, was the tomb built for the benefit of the community or was it for the benefit of those who initiated and oversaw the construction of the tomb?

Many archaeologists feel that the Neolithic burial rite although appearing to express the collective and thus the egalitarian nature of society, actually masks the reality that society was socially differentiated and argue that the ancestors were used as means of legitimising access to resources and positions of power. Thus the dead may have been anonymous in their burial chambers, but ultimately they ensured that a ruling class continued to occupy their position in society.

Also, it is well known that in many ancient States rulers used monuments as a means of impressing on their subjects their power and authority (as they also do in modern times). Of course, there was no Neolithic State but one is left with the feeling that Tan y Muriau long cairn was designed to impress. It is quite possible therefore, that this monuments was built by a élite and that it further reinforced and expressed their position amongst the Neolithic communities in this area.

### Building the tombs

One of the puzzles of the Neolithic period is how the people of this time built the stone tombs in which they deposited their dead. One only has to consider the huge capstone on the portal dolmen at Tan y Muriau to realise that there was skill, intelligence and sheer, physical power behind the construction of megalithic tombs (a capstone on a portal dolmen at Kernastown in Ireland weighs around 100 tons!).

It seems likely that teams of men and probably oxen also, transported the huge stones used for tombs, using ropes and timber sleds or rollers. In the actual construction of the tomb, the smaller supporting stones of chambers would have presented fewer problems and could have been raised using manpower, ropes and levers. However, raising and positioning the capstones would have caused major engineering problems. It is possible that capstones were pulled up earthen ramps or even part of the covering cairn. Another possibility is that they were lifted in stages using levers and timber platforms and scaffolding.

All the above methods are feasible, but the reality is that we have no real evidence that reveals the methods behind the construction of megalithic tombs. Therefore, we can only stand and wonder when we come to consider how they were built.

## Neolithic 'Churches'

In this chapter I have used the word 'tomb' to refer to the various funerary structures that were built by Neolithic people throughout Europe. However, it is surely the case that Neolithic tombs functioned on more than one level and were more than just places where the dead were buried. Neolithic tombs must have been central to the religious life of the communities of this time, and may have functioned in a similar way as the later parish churches of the medieval (and later) periods that were found in many rural parts of the British Isles.

Although we only have tantalising hints of the true nature of Neolithic religious beliefs, it seems likely that their tombs were also places were communities came to regularly participate in ritual ceremonies connected with their religion. Perhaps as Trevor Garnham has plausibly suggested, the Neolithic communities came to their tombs to call on the spirits of their forefathers rather than 'Our Father who art in Heaven'?

Evidence of these ceremonies has been found at a number of Neolithic tombs across the British Isles. At the impressive Cotswold-Severn tomb of Capel Garmon near Betws-y-Coed, fires were lit close to the passage in the tomb's side, while in the forecourt of another Cotswold-Severn tomb at Rodmarton (Glouc.), fires were also lit and the teeth of oxen, horses, and pigs were scattered. A human tooth and boar's tusks were also found in the forecourt and Aubrey Burl has provided us with an explanation for this evidence: 'Here surely, as the fires blazed, people had carried human and animal skulls, laying them down, using the human bones and the animal totems of the group in rites that were designed to bring health and good fortune to the community'. An imaginative rendering of the evidence no doubt, but one that is probably not that far from the truth.

One of the most fascinating pieces of evidence relating to rituals and ceremonies carried out at Neolithic tombs, was found at the well known passage grave of Barclodiad-y-Gawres on Yyns Môn. In the central chamber, a thick deposit of earth and charcoal was found. After this deposit had been scientifically analysed, it was found to contain the remains of oysters, limpets, wrasse, eel, whiting, frog, common and natterjack toads, grass snake, mouse, shrew and rabbit. It appears that a stew had been made from all of these creatures and had then been poured onto a fire after it had died down to its embers. Finally, small pebbles and shells were thrown onto this mixture. As Richard Sharkey nicely puts it in *The Meeting of the Tracks (Rock Art in Ancient Wales)*, '[t]he ritual sequence that was suggested with this ceremonial brew [was] worthy of Macbeth's three witches'.

We may even have some evidence for rituals taking place at one of the peninsula's tombs. A short note in **Archaeologia Cambrensis** 1926, mentions that the landowner, a Mr F. G. Wynn, had found a paving of cobbles in the chamber of the Bach wen tomb, which were blackened as if by fire. Admittedly however, this evidence could well be related to 'modern' fires being lit in the chamber, as it would make a convenient sheltering place.

## Chapter 3

# Mynydd Rhiw Neolithic Axe Factory

### The stone axe in Neolithic society

It is beyond doubt that the stone axe was the fundamental tool of the Neolithic period. It would have been used for many different tasks – from building houses to boats – and its importance in the creation of land suitable for agriculture cannot be unduly stressed. It is also evident that there was a darker side to the use of stone axes in Neolithic Europe and evidence of this is graphically provided by a discovery made in 1983, at Talheim in the Neckar Valley, Germany. Here, a man digging in his garden uncovered human remains and subsequent excavation of the site revealed a confused but well preserved mass of human bones, which represented at least 34 complete skeletons. Sherds of LBK pottery found among the bones indicated that this mass grave dated to c. 7000 BC and subsequent radiocarbon dates confirmed this.

It was evident that the people in the grave had been thrown carelessly into it, as many were lying in unnatural positions and this evidence contrasted strongly with the careful arrangements of single graves normally seen in LBK cemeteries. The apparent lack of respect accorded to the dead alerted the excavators that they were on to something sinister and the obvious signs of severe trauma on many of the skulls confirmed this. Over half of them showed that many must have died as a result of severe blows to the head, with the resulting holes being generally ovate in shape, 2-3 cm wide and several centimetres long. Tellingly, the shape of the injuries corresponds closely to the cross-sections of the stone axes used by the farmers of the LBK.

Similar evidence to that found at Talheim has been found at Schletz in Austria, which was a late LBK settlement that was surrounded by a double enclosure. Large numbers of skeletons were found in the bottom of the enclosure ditch (many of them lying face down) and as at Talheim it was apparent that many of the bodies had been thrown in haphazardly. The 67 skeletons recovered from the ditch all showed signs of violence and it was evident from some of the injuries that stone axes had again been used as lethal weapons.

What lay behind this deadly violence is unclear, but it may be that the emerging Neolithic lifestyle, with its emphasis on permanence, engendered strong feelings of territoriality among different groups and that sometimes this spiralled out of control into extreme violence. We will never know the truth but such evidence once again reminds us that man has engaged in conflict for many thousands of years and unfortunately, this will probably continue to be the case.

While it is obvious that stone axes were used for many practical tasks and also as weapons, it is clear that they had a significance that went beyond their everyday use. For instance, a beautiful and superbly made stone axe (which had never been used) was found beneath the Neolithic 'Sweet Track' during excavations in the Somerset Levels. This wooden trackway dates to 3807/6 BC and it allowed Neolithic people to cross some 2km of wet fen in the Somerset Levels (perhaps to a religious site). The axe, which had been laboriously ground and polished until it was finely shaped and exquisitely smooth, may have taken over 100 hours to complete. Of more interest however, is the fact that the axe was deliberately deposited in the water below the track and was made from a stone known as jadeite which is found in the Swiss or Italian Alps.

Many Neolithic axes have also been found in a short stretch of the Thames and for the most part they are in good condition and do not reveal much evidence of actual use. Many of these axes originated in axe 'factories' in the Lake District, Cornwall and northern Wales and again, we appear to have deliberate deposition in water.

Many ancient and 'primitive' societies venerated streams, rivers and other watery places as sacred places that were connected to the otherworld or underworld. In ancient Ireland, for example the Celtic tribes who lived near the River Boyne are said to have believed that the river flowed out of the otherworld from the sacred well of Segais, which watered the nine hazel trees of wisdom. It is quite possible that similar religious beliefs existed among Neolithic communities, though of course, these beliefs remain forever lost and we can only make assumptions from the evidence that is available to us. Nevertheless, whatever the reality behind their beliefs, the evidence does suggest that Neolithic people viewed water in a similar way to their Iron Age descendants. Indeed, as well as appearing to deliberately deposit their stone axes in watery places, it is evident that many Neolithic monuments in the British Isles are located close to rivers and it seems that there is some religious connection between them.

This practice of making deliberate offerings in water (known to archaeologists as 'votive deposits') continued into the Bronze and Iron Ages and it should be mentioned here that votive deposits were also placed in the ground from the Neolithic to the Iron Age (and perhaps also in earlier prehistoric periods). It is probable that prehistoric people believed that these places were the haunts of supernatural powers that were to be both respected and feared, and so, such offerings may have been made in order to ask for their help or to placate them. It should also be pointed out here, that some of the Mesolithic finds that have come from watery places may actually have been votive deposits rather than accidental losses.

It is also evident that finely made stone axes were deliberately deposited at Neolithic monuments. For example, a jadeite axe and axes of Cornish greenstone were buried at one of the three enclosures found inside the huge Neolithic earthwork at Hambledon Hill in Dorset, while a concentration of axes was found near the famous standing stone near Rudston, Yorkshire (at over 25ft high this is the tallest monolith in the British Isles). A greenstone axe (probably from Cornwall) was also found beneath the Altar Stone at Stonehenge and in Ireland a beautiful axe made from diorite was deposited in the forecourt of the court-cairn (a type of megalithic tomb found in Ireland) at Creevykeel, Co. Sligo. Near Perth Chwarau in Clwyd, a cave had been used as a Neolithic burial place and outside its entrance a stone axe had been buried. At nearby Gop, an unused stone axe was set upright outside another cave that had also been used as a Neolithic sepulchre. Aubrey Burl has made the interesting suggestion that some of the stone axes deposited at Neolithic monuments and tombs personified a female guardian who watched over the dead.

Similar practices have been observed on the continent and for example at the Neolithic tomb of Manio in Brittany, five polished axes were buried at the base of a standing stone that also featured strange engravings of what looked like sinuous serpents. Nearby at the tomb of Mané er Hroek, axe carvings were made on stones within the tomb and around a hundred fine diorite and jadeite axes also accompanied the deceased placed within the burial chamber.

**Factories and Mines**
The rock and flint used to make Neolithic stone axes and other artefacts, came from a number of sources, with the most readily available being the rock and flint that could be found lying on the surface. The most productive sources however, were the axe factories and flint mines that were opened up by Neolithic communities (underground flint is of a superior quality because it has not been subjected to weakening by frosts). Before the axe factory at Mynydd Rhiw is discussed, we will look briefly at some of these fascinating sites.

The sites of several Neolithic axe factories have been identified in the British Isles and important factories are found at Great Langdale in the Lake District, Penmaenmawr in Gwynedd and Mounts Bay in Cornwall. Among other places, axe factories are also found at Tievebulliagh in County Antrim, Killin in Perthshire and in the Preseli Mountains in south-western Wales. The famous setting of standing stones known as the 'bluestones', which can still be seen today at Stonehenge, are very likely to have originated in the Preseli mountains in Pembrokeshire.

What is intriguing is that that many of these factories are located in dramatic and remote spots in the landscape. At Great Langdale, the axe factory was located on the upper slopes of a high fell known as the Pike O' Stickle, while at Penmaenmawr the material was quarried high on the headland of Graig Llwyd. It is still possible to see a distinct notch in Graig Llwyd, which marks the Neolithic quarry and reveals that extraction of rock was on a substantial scale. Such sites reveal that even though suitable stone for axes could be acquired more easily elsewhere, Neolithic people deliberately exploited rock at striking but more inaccessible locations in the landscape. As will be seen below, the axe factory at Mynydd Rhiw also seems to conform to this pattern.

It would not be stretching the bounds of credibility to suggest that to the Neolithic mind, places such as Pike O' Stickle and Graig Llwyd were seen as sacred and special parts of the landscape. It is surely no coincidence that as mentioned above, the Stonehenge bluestones originated in the Preseli mountains, where there was also a Neolithic axe factory. These huge stones were transported some two hundred miles to Salisbury Plain and their inclusion in what must have been the major religious monument of the British Isles during the Early Bronze Age, lends credence to the idea that the Neolithic axe factories were located in sacred areas of the landscape.

The exact reasoning behind the Neolithic conception of these places is lost to us, but it is probable that they were seen as the domain of powerful forces – perhaps ancestral sprits or gods of the natural world. As Gabriel Cooney has pointed out 'in many different societies peaks have a special quality as sacred places because they seem to touch the sky, and are seen as the seat of the gods'. It is also interesting to note that the Preseli mountains lie west of Salisbury Plain and in many ancient and 'primitive' societies the west, where the sun goes down, is considered to be the land of the dead. As Mike Pitts has said (in his superb book, Hengeworld) of the bluestones, '[t]hose extraordinary alien megaliths assembled at Stonehenge [were] brought from beyond the setting horizon, from the place where ancestors live and the dead travel, to meet the new dead in the land of the living'.

Therefore, it seems quite likely that Neolithic people believed that axes quarried at the axe factories contained some sort of sacred power and thus were greatly desired by communities, which lay far from the factories. There is some ethnographic evidence which hints at Neolithic beliefs regarding the nature of the places in which they quarried (and mined) stone. The Tungei people of New Guinea, for example, felt that only 'ritually pure' people could quarry the stone needed for their axes as these people would not 'upset' the sprit guardians of the stone. Even in more modern times similar beliefs can be recognised. In Ireland, it was a tradition not to dig or disturb the ground on certain days of the year as it was felt dangerous to disturb the sprits who were more active during these occasions. Such evidence as the above, perhaps helps in our efforts to understand why a stone axe that originated in the Alps ended up in the Somerset Levels, why many Langdale axes are found in Lincolnshire, or why axes from Graig Llwyd are found in the Thames, the Peak District and Yorkshire.

It is possible to discover the sources from which such axes originated because of 'petrological analysis'. This involves cutting a small sample from an axe and this is then ground down to a slice that is thousandths of a millimetre thick. This slice is then examined under a microscope and matched to known geological specimens that have been mapped by the British geological survey (which is of a very high standard). Six definite axe factories have been identified in Wales, though there are likely to have been several more and the axes produced at them show a homogeneity in form, which varies little for some two thousand years.

It may be convenient to refer to the places where Neolithic axes were produced in some numbers as 'factories', but we should not lose sight of the fact that this is a term relevant to our world, rather than that of the Neolithic. Mark Edmonds, who is an authority on flint and stone working in prehistoric Britain, feels that we need to be careful when using such terms as 'factory', as they 'carry with them sociological implications which need to be demonstrated rather than assumed'. He has also pointed out that the extraction of rock may have been sporadic and small-scale but over a lengthy period of time and John Wadell in Prehistoric Ireland notes a similar situation at the Irish axe factories. This perhaps reinforces the idea that Neolithic people viewed axe factories as sacred places, rather than places of a more 'industrial' nature.

As mentioned above, it was not just the axe factories that provided suitable material for Neolithic stone axes, but also mines. The most famous Neolithic flint mine has to be Grime's Graves in Norfolk, which was in use from the late Neolithic to the Early Bronze Age (c. 3000-2000 BC). The prehistoric miners at Grime's Graves dug over 400 shafts in order to reach the narrow bands of flint that lay below ground in the chalk.

The best quality flint, both in terms of its working qualities and appearance (a dark, shiny flint known as floorstone) lay deep underground and in some cases, the miners had to sink shafts of up to 15m to reach the floorstone. From the bottom of the shafts the miners dug a series of interconnecting galleries that followed the seams of flint. The tools used in mining consisted of picks made from red deer antler and ox shoulder blades and shaped pieces of wood were used as shovels. Working down the mine cannot have been particularly easy with work being carried out in conditions that must have been hot, stuffy and often cramped. Although none have been found at Grime's Graves, it seems likely that miners worked by the light of small chalk lamps containing animal fat. Carbon stains from these lamps have been found on the walls and roofs of other Neolithic mines. It is possible also, that daylight shining down the shafts and reflecting off the chalk, gave the miners enough light to work by once their eyes had become used to its low intensity.

Other Neolithic flint mines are known in England and include sites such as Harrow Hill or Cissbury in Sussex and at least another ten are known. With the exception of Grime's Graves the English flint mines are in locations that provide superb views and it is likely that as with the axe factories, it was more than just the availability of suitable material that led Neolithic miners to these places in the landscape.

## The Mynydd Rhiw axe factory

If you were walking past it today, unless you knew it was there, you would almost certainly miss the Neolithic axe factory on the headland of Mynydd Rhiw. All you would see under the dwarf gorse that virtually covers the headland are indistinct hollows, which run in a line across the north end of the hill. To the untrained eye these hollows may look like natural undulations but they actually represent the remains of the Neolithic quarry workings. There are five quarrying areas but one appears to have now become covered over with gorse and is no longer visible.

Although this site lacks the immediate impact of the megalithic tombs of the peninsula it does, in a way, bring us even closer to the Neolithic people who lived here. If you were to stop, and braving the prickly gorse, search among the hollows, you would find evidence that around 6000 years ago people sat here and made stone axes and other tools. This evidence takes the form of various-sized angular chunks of fine-grained and flinty rock, which represent the waste material from the production of the above implements. This debris provides us with a remarkable connection to an ancient people who lived lives that were both similar and alien to our own.

The axe factory on the headland of Mynydd Rhiw, like many of its counterparts elsewhere in the British Isles, is located in a remote and dramatic part of the landscape and the possible significance of this has been discussed above. It is situated near the summit of Mynydd Rhiw on its north-eastern slopes and the views from here are superb, with the patchwork fields of Llŷn unfolding in front of you towards Garn Fadrun, Yr Eifl and the headland of Mynydd Cilan jutting out into the Irish Sea.

C.H. Houlder and his team excavated the Mynydd Rhiw axe factory in a two-week period during September 1958. In total, six excavations were undertaken (sites A-G) and the team found firm evidence for the manufacture of stone axes and other Neolithic tools. They also discovered that the majority of the axes and other tools had not been made from outcrops of visible rock, (as is the case at other axe factories in the British Isles), but that that Neolithic people had skilfully targeted seams of shale below the surface. It was evident that at first, Neolithic people had sporadically used fragments of the shale bedrock that lay on the hillside, but at some point, they had realised that this good quality rock was found in a seam that ran below the hillside and they

*Y Ffôr (1)*

*Cefn Isaf (2)*

*Bach Wen (3)*

*Mynydd Cefnamwlch (4)*

*Tan y Muriau (5)*

*Tan y Muriau (6)*

*Ystum Cegid Isaf (7)*

*Bronheulog (8)*

*Penarth (9)*

*Mynydd Cilan (10)*

*Site of Mynydd Rhiw axe factory (11)*

*Mynydd Rhiw from Afon Soch (12)*

*From axe factory,*
*Mynydd Rhiw (13)*

*Axe from Mynydd Rhiw (14)*

*Hafted axe from Anglesey (14a)*

*Sarn Mellteyrn (15)*

*Llangwnnadl (16)*

*Pandy Saethon (16a)*

*Nant y Gledrydd (17)*          *Yr Eifl (17a)*

*Tir Gwyn (18, 19)*

*Trallwyn (20)*          *Cefngraeanog (21)*

*Glynllifon (22)*

*Tyddyn Mawr (24)*

*Betws Fawr (23)*

*Tir Bach (25)*

*Tir Bach (26)*          *Capel Tan y Foel (27)*

*Bodfan (28)*

*Bodfan (29)*          *Glan Afon (36)*

*Glasfryn (30, 31, 32, 32a)*

*Gyrn Ddu (33)*    *Gyrn Ddu (34)*

*Morfa Abererch (35)*    *Plas ym Mhenllech (37)*

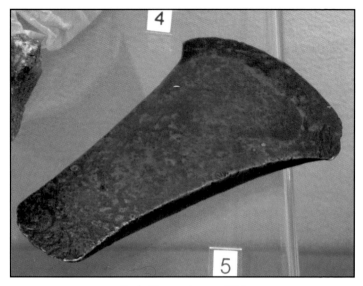

*Early Bronze Age axe (38)*

*Llithfaen Beaker (39)*          *Battle axe from Chwilog (40)*

*Mynydd Carnguwch (41)*

*Tre'r Ceiri (42)*

*Yr Eifl (43-45)*

subsequently, quarried it. Some of the quarry pits reached 3m deep and so in a way, the axe factory was almost a mine. The 'miners' however abandoned the quarry pits as each one started to get too deep for comfort and these dangerous pits were filled in using the spoil from the new ones.

## The Domestic Industry and Factory Products

Although the production of stone axes was the chief concern of the Neolithic workforce at Mynydd Rhiw, other tools were produced, some of which relate to daily activities at the site. As Houlder points out in the excavation report, even if the axe factory was only a working site and Neolithic people did not live here, stone tools would have been needed for such things as food preparation and the making of other objects used at the site. Houlder classified such tools as belonging to the 'domestic industry' while the stone axes and knives that were made for use away from Mynydd Rhiw are known as 'factory products'.

Many of the domestic tools were found lying around the remains of two hearths where Neolithic people had lit fires. These hearths were discovered in the earliest part of the quarry which, once redundant, became filled with waste and a hollow was formed where Neolithic workers could shelter. It seems likely that as well as providing warmth (because of the strong winds that often whip across the exposed headland it can get cold on Mynydd Rhiw even in the summer), food was also prepared on these fires. It is also possible that sticks used to help in the extraction of rock were hardened in these fires.

The domestic tools were produced on the smaller pieces of stone (known as waste flakes or 'debitage') that had been detached from larger pieces of rock ('cores'), as they were being 'knapped' into axes and other tools. The knapping process required not only a great deal of skill, but also good knowledge of the fracturing qualities of various rocks. Small hammerstones made from various rocks and hammers made from antler and bone would have been used in the knapping process.

These waste flakes would have provided the Neolithic workforce on Mynydd Rhiw with convenient and very effective raw material for tools for daily tasks. Some six thousands years later, some of these flakes still have very sharp edges and can easily cut a finger. If you are fortunate enough to be on Mynydd Rhiw when the gorse has been burnt back, you will be able to find some of these flakes, along with the larger pieces of waste material, when otherwise they be hard to find (please remember that they should not be taken from the site).

The domestic tools found during the excavations consisted of knives, scrapers, burins and awls. Scrapers would have been used for the preparation of animal hides, while burins and awls would have been used for piercing bone and other materials. Such tools were made by modifying or 'retouching' the ends and the sides of the flakes in various ways, though there were also many flakes that had not undergone any retouch and were simply used as they were found. Mention should also be made of the large hammerstones that were used by the Neolithic quarrymen to extract the shale bedrock from the quarry pits. The hammerstones discovered during excavations mostly consisted of nodules of rock (dolerite) found on the hill and it was also apparent that a few hammerstones had been gathered from the rocky beach at Porth Neigwl.

Turning now to the factory products made at the site, we will begin with the stone axes, because as mentioned previously, they would have been the prime concern of the Neolithic toolmakers at Mynydd Rhiw. There seems to have been two types of axe made at Mynydd Rhiw – those that were somewhat narrow and thin in section and the sturdier and heavier axes which were oval in section. It appears that there was a bias towards the lighter axes, which also showed greater diversity in shape. Houlder suggested that the lighter axes may have been made for more delicate woodworking activities, while the heavier axes were used for tree-felling. No finished axes were found during excavations, which suggests that the grinding and polishing – which made stone axes more effective as tools and more aesthetically pleasing – took place somewhere else. This was often the case at Neolithic axe factories where activity was concentrated on producing 'rough-outs', which were then taken away from site to be ground and polished (the Mynydd Rhiw axes were often only polished on their edges).

It should also be remembered that stone axes produced at Mynydd Rhiw are likely to have carried with them a deeper symbolism that was somehow connected to the Neolithic conception of Mynydd Rhiw as a sacred place. It is worth pointing out here, that along with the Neolithic tombs of Tan y Muriau and Bronheulog, there is also a cairn cemetery of the Early Bronze Age found on the slopes of Mynydd Rhiw. It is also known that a small stone circle once existed on the lower slopes of Mynydd Rhiw near Meillionydd (recorded by the antiquarian Edward Lhwyd in 1696), but unfortunately, this has since been destroyed. It has been suggested by a number of scholars that stone circles were places where trade in Neolithic axes took place and it is perhaps possible that the stone circle recorded by Lhwyd functioned in a similar way, with 'outsiders' coming to trade for the Mynydd Rhiw axes.

Such evidence as the above strongly suggests that Mynydd Rhiw was sacred to Neolithic and Early Bronze Age communities and because of this, they not only buried their dead here and erected other ritual and ceremonial monuments, but also came to quarry its rock. It may well be that this prehistoric conception of Mynydd Rhiw had a long heritage that stretched back into the Mesolithic and perhaps even further back in time.

As mentioned above, knives were also made at Mynydd Rhiw and like the stone axes, Houlder classed them as factory products that were destined for use elsewhere in the peninsula and beyond. The knives were made on large flakes that were detached from prepared 'cores' of shale. By carefully shaping these cores prior to flake removal, the Neolithic tool makers at Mynydd Rhiw were able to predetermine the shape of the flakes that were struck from them and thus they were able to produce two main types of knife – lunate and discoidal.

## Mynydd Rhiw and the Axe 'Trade'

Many of the Neolithic axes and tools made at the Mynydd Rhiw factory must have been used by local Neolithic groups in the peninsula (e.g. the axe found near Sarn Bach, in Llŷn). However, it is evident that as with many stone axes found in the British Isles, some of those from Mynydd Rhiw ended up far from their place of origin. For example, Mynydd Rhiw axes have been found near Beddgelert in the heart of Snowdonia, on Ynys Môn, at Llanegryn in Meirionnydd and at Craswall Priory in Herefordshire.

Such evidence shows that Neolithic people were carrying axes long distances from the factories and some archaeologists feel that this indicates a Neolithic axe trade that was organised along similar lines to that of a modern market economy. For instance, C.H. Houlder in the Mynydd Rhiw excavation report, talks about 'consumers' (who he identifies as lowland farmers) and 'middle-men' who were the 'real traders who knew what was needed by the consumer, and also knew where to get it'. However, many archaeologists are turning away from this interpretation of the Neolithic axe trade, which suggests that there were Neolithic 'merchants' who were in charge of the axe trade. Joshua Pollard, for example, has suggested that down-the-line exchange (stone axes simply being passed from one individual to another in hand-to-hand exchanges) is the most likely mechanism behind the Neolithic axe trade. He feels that stone axes from the factories were used to reinforce bonds and alliances between different communities and also as an expression of status by certain individuals. This last suggestion carries some weight when we consider the evidence discussed above; a stone axe acquired by an individual from a distant and revered source may have meant this person was accorded a greater level of respect in their community. Although this interpretation does not disprove the fact that axes from the axe factories were certainly used in practical tasks, it seems likely that axes always carried with them a level of religious symbolism that was related to their place of origin. Mark Edmonds has also pointed out that archaeological analysis of the distribution of stone axes in Britain, indicates that they were circulated in hand-to-hand exchanges which took place over hundreds of years.

Nevertheless we still cannot totally disregard the

existence of a Neolithic axe trade that was more akin to trade, as we would perceive it. Frances Lynch has pointed out in the absorbing Prehistoric Wales, that large numbers of Neolithic axes from different factories have been found in the Flintshire hills near Prestatyn and at Merthyr Mawr Warren on the Pembrokeshire coast. She points out that these axes may have been gathered together for 'export' and that this evidence lends support to those who favour a more 'commercial' axe trade. Also chips from Mynydd Rhiw axes have been found at both these sites, which suggests that the final polishing and grinding of axes may have occurred here – perhaps lending further support to the commercial interpretation of the axe trade. As with many other aspects of the Neolithic, there is some debate as to the true nature of the Neolithic axe trade, but it seems possible that it varied from place to place because of the different needs of the 'consumers'.

An intriguing question concerning the axe factory at Mynydd Rhiw is – who were the people who worked here? Firstly, we know that stone from the slopes of Mynydd Rhiw was being worked in the earlier Neolithic because around 4000 BC, a pendant made from Mynydd Rhiw stone was found in an early Neolithic context in the Dyffryn Ardudwy tomb. However, this pendant could have been made by people of Mesolithic origin or by Neolithic immigrants and brings us no closer to the identity of the people who worked here. Evidence found on Anglesey however, perhaps suggests that it may have been people of a hunter-gatherer ancestry who were responsible for the axe factory at Mynydd Rhiw. This evidence takes the form of flakes of Mynydd Rhiw stone that were found at the Mesolithic site of Trwyn Du on the island. Although these flakes would have come from raw material that was taken from the surface of Mynydd Rhiw during the Mesolithic, they suggest perhaps, that in the Neolithic, native people of Mesolithic origin sought out and further exploited this source of good quality rock.

C.H. Houlder also made the suggestion that the axe factory at Mynydd Rhiw was worked by people whose roots lay in the indigenous Mesolithic population. He pointed out that many of the domestic tools found at the site were those that would have been more useful for hunting and that a larger proportion of the axes produced were of the lighter variety, with most of the heavier ones being traded. This may indicate that the people who worked at Mynydd Rhiw were semi-agricultural and did not require the heavier axes, which would have been more useful for a farming lifestyle of a more permanent nature.

Whether the people responsible for the axe factory on Mynydd Rhiw were of Mesolithic ancestry or were Neolithic newcomers does not really matter and the reality, is that we shall probably never know the answer to this question. What is important about the axe factory at Mynydd Rhiw, is the fact that it opens a small but remarkable window onto the daily lives of people who lived and worked in this quiet corner of the peninsula, some six thousand years ago.

## Chapter 4

# Introduction to the Early Bronze Age

Life for many of the people who lived in the British Isles in the Early Bronze Age (c. 2500-1500 BC) would not have been radically different from that of their Neolithic predecessors. Nevertheless, during this time there were technological and social changes that mark a significant departure from the preceding Neolithic period. One of these changes was the introduction of metallurgy, which must surely rank as one of the most pivotal events in the course of human history.

At a basic level, metallurgy can be described as the practice of turning metal ores into useable objects. The earliest metalworking may come from the site of Çayönü Tepesi in southern Turkey, where copper objects dating to c. 7000 BC have been discovered. These artefacts however, had been made from 'pure' copper, which had been taken straight from the host rock and hammered into shape. This was a convenient way of making metal goods but left them brittle and thus easily damaged.

By the end of the Fifth millennium BC in Europe, 'true' metallurgy, which involved the smelting of copper ores in fires of a very high temperature was established and the well known copper mines at Aibunar in Bulgaria and Rudna Glava in Yugoslavia date to this time. By 2500 BC, the metallurgical process – which must have been viewed with awe by many – had arrived in the British Isles and metal objects were being seen for the first time.

The Early Bronze Age in the British Isles also saw the establishment of new religious monuments and burial practices and it is apparent that these were also introduced into the peninsula. In Chapters 5, 6 and 7 we will examine the new monuments and burials of the Early Bronze Age in the peninsula and discuss what 'messages' they may impart to the modern observer. Before we do so however, evidence relating to the more prosaic aspects of life in the peninsula during the Early Bronze Age will be examined.

The climate of the peninsula during this time would not have differed greatly from that of the preceding Neolithic. Summers, though, would have been warmer and drier and although the winters were probably more severe, they were probably still milder than many other parts of the British Isles (as they continue to be today).

Pollen sequences from the Early Bronze Age in Wales, reveal that the people of this time were making changes to the environment in which they lived and that upland forests were being cleared to make way for agriculture. The use of the uplands for agricultural purposes during this period perhaps suggests that good farming land in the lowlands was becoming overused because of a rising human population and this led to new land being sought out.

Although the Early Bronze Age farming economy is not completely understood, it does seem likely it was pastoral in nature and that the uplands of Wales were used as grazing areas during the kinder summer months. On the basis of the archaeological evidence, cattle seem to have been the dominant animal in this economy and it is also likely that sheep were not uncommon on farms of the Early Bronze Age. Also, as Frances Lynch has pointed out, the red deer of the uplands would have provided another natural resource for the farmers of this time (as they must have done for their earlier predecessors).

Unfortunately, the evidence for Early Bronze farms in upland Wales remains inconclusive, though it seems probable that some of the prehistoric settlements found in many parts of Wales (though they are rare in the south) date to this period. The remains of prehistoric settlements survive in many parts of the peninsula and likewise, some of these are likely to represent farms of the Early Bronze Age.

Whether some of the Early Bronze Age farms in the Welsh uplands were occupied year-round remains open to debate because conditions in the winter would not have been particularly favourable in this respect. Nevertheless, it is a possibility that cannot be totally discounted and continuing archaeological research will hopefully make things clearer.

There is however, some firmer evidence for arable farming in the lowlands of Early Bronze Age Wales and this comes from Stackpole Warren in Pembrokeshire. Although the picture of the Early Bronze Age settlement here is muddied by later occupation and activity at the site, a large-round house dating to c. 2000 BC was excavated. The house seems to have originally consisted of a light, wooden structure that was replaced (after the former had burned down) by the more substantial round-house with featured large internal posts and a wall measuring 6.5 metres in diameter.

Finds from the house comprised of a number of sherds from Beakers and Collared Urns – types of pottery characteristic of the Early Bronze Age. A fine example of a Collared urn was found near Rhiw, in Llŷn and can be seen in the illustration. Flint tools animal bones and cereal grains (mainly barley) were also found and plough-marks discovered nearby may mark the existence of a field contemporary with the early Bronze Age settlement at Stackpole Warren.

Pollen sequences have been recovered from the peninsula (Llŷn) and have revealed that although the people of the Early Bronze Age were having an impact on its landscape, woodland clearances in the lowlands were fairly modest in scale. In the uplands however, it appears that even at this early stage of deforestation soils were being degraded by their exposure to the elements. This process eventually led to the formation of blanket peats in many upland regions in Late Bronze Age Wales.

Studies of skeletal remains from the Early Bronze tell a similar story to those of the Neolithic and reveal that life was far from comfortable for Early Bronze Age communities. For instance, several adults and children were discovered in an Early Bronze Age grave on Overton Down, Wiltshire; it was noticed on examination of the bones that some of the children had suffered from malnutrition. In 1915, a flat grave dating to the Early Bronze Age was discovered in the same area at Upavon flying school. It contained the remains of an elderly man who had suffered from rheumatoid arthritis of the spine (which led to its curvature) and who also had many abscesses in his teeth. It is apparent that poor dental hygiene was common among these people and gum disease and toothache must have plagued them.

In Scotland, studies of bones found in graves dating to the Early Bronze Age revealed that around half the men lived beyond 36 years, while around 85 per cent of the women died before they reached 25. It is likely, as Aubrey Burl has pointed out in his engrossing book, The Stonehenge People that this was due to inferior diet and childbirth.

It is worth noting here that the above skeletal evidence comes from graves dating to the 'Beaker period' in the British Isles (c. 2500-2000 BC). This period takes its name from the finely decorated pots or Beakers, that along with other novel items, accompanied single burials that were usually, but not exclusively, male. The deceased were placed under mounds of earth or stone (barrows and cairns), often in pits or 'cist' graves (rectangular stone boxes) and in some cases, Beaker burials were simply placed in flat graves and were not covered by burial mounds. The bodies in Beaker burials were often placed in the graves lying on their sides in a crouched or 'foetal' position, with the legs flexed and the knees drawn up towards the chest.

It should also be pointed out that although the 'typical' Beaker burial often consisted of a single person accompanied by distinctive grave goods, beaker burials containing several people are also known. However, even in Beaker graves containing several people, the emphasis was still placed on the individual and it is possible to recognise separate acts of burial in multiple Beaker burials. This is in contrast to the collective burials of the Neolithic tombs where individual identity was lost through the mixing together of the bones of the dead.

The widespread distribution of Beaker burials throughout Europe in the mid to latter half of the third millennium BC, led earlier archaeologists to propose the concept of the 'Beaker people', who migrated from their homeland in Iberia or Central Europe to other parts of the Continent and the British Isles.

Earlier archaeologists also felt that one of the main driving forces behind the Beaker migrations was the search for Metal ores and that the Beaker people introduced metalworking to parts of Western Europe such as Britain and

Ireland because of the occurrence of novel metal artefacts in Beaker graves. It was also felt that the Beaker people came to dominate the indigenous societies in the areas they settled in because of their knowledge of the secrets of metalworking and because a powerful warrior aristocracy led them. However, in recent years the traditional view has been under increasing critical pressure and the Beaker people are no longer seen as a culturally distinct group of people. Rather, the appearance of the Beaker 'package' is, as Aubrey Burl has succinctly said, 'explained by the adoption of a new system of beliefs which brought with it new paraphernalia'.

Nevertheless, recent discoveries from the British Isles suggest that there is more than a little truth in the original concept of the Beaker people and that we should perhaps be wary of the vagaries of archaeological fashion. As Mike Pitts says of the recent refutation of the original concept of the Beaker people, '[t]he possibility that at this time in Europe certain people were on the move, in search of land and other resources, needs to be revisited'. These discoveries will be discussed in Chapter 6, where we will look at the archaeological evidence for the Beaker people in the Peninsula.

As mentioned above, metallurgy first appeared in the British Isles around 2500 BC and in Wales, simple, flat copper axes were the earliest metal artefacts. Although these axes are scarce we do have some fine examples, such as the three found in the hoard from Moel Arthur in the Clwydian Hills. A flat axe has also been found on the slopes of Tre'r Ceiri in Llŷn. Stylistic similarities and chemical analysis of these early Welsh axes strongly suggest that they were imports from Ireland. Indeed, as Paul Budd has pointed out the early flat axes from not only Wales but also England and Scotland, 'share the distinctive arsenic, antimony and silver impurity pattern' of flat axes from Munster.

Such evidence shows how prehistoric metallurgy originated in Ireland and that Irish workshops dominated the earliest stage of metalworking in Britain and Ireland. This is important because as we shall see later, the birth of metallurgy in Ireland is also tied in with the appearance of the Beaker people here.

However, it was not long before the emphasis had shifted from Ireland to Britain and by 2000 BC, smiths in Britain had made a hugely important step in the development of metallurgy in Europe and began producing artefacts made from a standardised bronze alloy of around 90% copper and 10% tin. This mixing of copper ores with tin during the smelting process gave the tools and weapons produced a more durable quality than those items made only from copper.

The tin needed for such items was imported from places further afield such as Brittany. It seems almost certain that Cornwall was also a rich source of tin in the Bronze Age, even though no tin mines dating to this period have yet been found here (destruction caused by later workings and erosion of the coastline could account for this). Nevertheless, it is possible that evidence of Bronze Age tin mining will one day, eventually be found in Cornwall.

Tin from Cornwall and Brittany would have been transported along the western seaways, which in effect formed a 'trading corridor' from Iberia to Scotland, along which goods (and ideas) were traded and exchanged during the prehistoric period. It was archaeologists working in the early 20th century who first revealed that the distribution pattern of artefacts along the western seaways could be explained by prehistoric trade. O.G.S. Crawford's 1936 paper – 'The Western Seaways' and Sir Cyril Fox's The Personality of Britain, published in 1932, stand out in this respect.

It is also undeniable that some prehistoric people must have migrated to new lands along this maritime 'highway' and we have already seen a probable example of this when discussing the inception of the Neolithic in the peninsula. The western seaways also played a significant part in the arrival of Christianity into the British Isles, which will be discussed in more detail in Chapter 10, when the archaeology of Early Christianity in the peninsula is examined.

The unifying nature of the Atlantic seaways even led in 1989 to the creation of a commission known as the 'Arc Atlantique', which includes all the countries and regions found along the western periphery of Europe and stretches from Spain to Scotland. Many of these countries and regions could be said to belong to the 'Celtic fringe' where ancient Celtic languages such as Welsh – which is derived from the original language of the ancient British Celts – are still spoken.

Many items of goldwork were produced during in the British Isles during the Early Bronze Age and some of the artefacts are spectacular. The Beaker period in particular is noted for fine goldwork and the objects produced during this time will be examined more closely in Chapter 6, which is concerned with the evidence for the Beaker people in the peninsula.

Mention should be made here of the fabulous and unique gold 'cape' that was discovered near Mold in 1833. This is one of the most impressive examples of Bronze Age goldwork from the British Isles and indeed is one of the finest examples of prehistoric goldwork from Europe. It was found with the skeleton of a young man, who had been laid to rest beneath a round barrow situated near the River Alun, just outside Mold in north-eastern Wales. The cape, which was superbly decorated had been beaten from a single piece of sheet gold and would have been worn across the shoulders. The holes that can be seen around the neck and bottom edge, which revealed that it had been attached to an inner lining of some sort, proved this. Even in its original condition it would have been a delicate object and must only have been worn on ceremonial occasions by a person of very high status, when it must have made a powerful impression on those who saw it. The cape may well date to the Early Bronze Age, rather than the Late Bronze Age as previously thought.

One area of the British Isles which is notable for its Early Bronze Age goldwork, is the Wessex region of southern England (particularly Wiltshire), where some of the most beautiful and finely made gold ornaments from prehistoric Europe have been found. The most famous of these were discovered under the earthen burial mound known as 'Bush Barrow', which lies close to Stonehenge. In 1808, the antiquarians William Cunnington and Sir Richard Colt Hoare dug a shaft through the barrow from top to bottom and although this method of excavation represented little more than treasure hunting, they nevertheless uncovered one of the most celebrated finds in British archaeology.

Lying beneath the barrow, they discovered the skeleton of a robust and tall man who had been buried with several fine objects – some of them of a superb quality – which marked him out as a person of high status. Among the collection of grave goods were three large bronze daggers, one of which was destroyed during the 'excavation'. Nevertheless, one of the surviving daggers featured workmanship of a quality that even a modern goldsmith would find hard to surpass. Its wooden handle had been decorated with thousands of tiny, inlaid gold pins, which formed a zigzag pattern, and it must have taken a great amount of time, skill and patience to complete. Aubrey Burl has suggested that the craftsman, to aid him in his work, may have used crystal or quartz as a magnifying instrument, or more probably, he was very short-sighted.

Also accompanying the man into the next world was a gold 'belt-hook' and two lozenge-shaped plaques of finely beaten, sheet gold. These were beautiful objects that had been skilfully decorated with clean and graceful lines and it seems likely that the plaques were originally attached to the man's clothing (which had long since disintegrated) as they featured small holes. It has been suggested that the decoration on the larger of the two gold plaques represent an idealised map of the Stonehenge landscape and that the man buried in Bush Barrow was the 'architect' of Stonehenge and was responsible for the erection of the circle of 'trilithons' (the huge uprights and lintels which form the main part of the monument). Others feel that it represents some type of solar or lunar calendar. While the plaque may possibly be some type of calendar or map (though it seems rather unlikely), radiocarbon dating indicates that the trilithons were put up several centuries before the burial of the Stonehenge 'architect'.

The Bush Barrow burial belongs to a group of around 100 richly furnished barrow burials which are found in the Wessex region of south-eastern England, with those containing gold (around 20), concentrated in north Wiltshire.

This has led some archaeologists to talk of a Gold Age' in Wessex and to suggest that they mark the burials of an intrusive warrior aristocracy known as the 'Wessex Culture', which was first defined in 1938 by the famous British prehistorian Stuart Piggot.

It was felt that the 'Wessex Culture' originated in Brittany because of stylistic and technical similarities seen on the goldwork found in contemporary barrow burials in this region. For instance, a number of the Breton Graves contain sheet gold ornaments and bronze daggers with handles decorated with geometric patterns of gold pins. Some of these daggers are very similar to the pair found in Bush Barrow. However, there are very few actual objects of Breton origin in the Wessex graves and it seems more likely that native leaders imitated their counterparts in Brittany with whom they were in contact through trade and exchange networks (though we cannot completely rule out kinship links between the two areas).

What is intriguing, is that detailed analysis of the Wessex goldwork strongly suggests that a single individual was responsible for most, if not all of the goldwork that was found in the Wessex Graves. It seems to be the case, then, that we have a master goldsmith who was 'plying his trade' among the Early Bronze Age 'nobles' on both sides of the channel.

## Copper mines of the Early Bronze Age in Wales

It is obvious that Wales played a very important part in the development of prehistoric metallurgy in the British Isles (and Europe) and it has a number of copper mines which originated in the Early Bronze Age. These mines provide us with fascinating evidence relating to the working methods employed in extracting copper ore in Bronze Age Wales and the Great Orme near Llandudno, in northern Wales is one of the most spectacular Bronze Age mines in Europe

Bronze Age mining at the Great Orme was on a huge scale with mine workings covering some 24,000 square metres and underground passages totalling around 6km. Mining at the site began around 1800 BC (or perhaps earlier) and ended c. 900 BC. It has been calculated that over 40, 000 cubic metres of rock were extracted during the search for copper ore during the Bronze Age. The soft or 'dolomitised' rock that surrounded the copper ores can help explain the size of the workings, but nevertheless the mine reveals the sophistication, efficiency and sheer effort of the prehistoric miners who once worked here. It is plain that the Great Orme must have been one of the major producers of copper in Bronze Age Europe

The artefacts found in the exploration of the prehistoric mine reveal how the miners set about the task of removing the copper ore from its bedrock. Around a thousand hammerstones have been found and these rounded glacial cobbles, some of which were very large, were used to remove the harder areas of rock in the mine. Many of the hammerstones were hand-held though small numbers were also hafted on to handles. Thousands of animal bones have also been discovered during investigations at the mine and mostly belong to cattle, pig and sheep, though some antler is also represented. While some of this skeletal evidence comes from food waste, it is obvious that many bones were shaped into points or picks, so that they could be used in mining the copper ore from the soft rock.

One intriguing question raised by the mine, is who actually worked in the underground shafts and galleries? Today, it is possible to visit some of the underground workings of the Bronze Age mine and a visit to the mine is thoroughly recommended. One is immediately struck by the cramped and narrow confines of many of the underground workings and as Frances Pryor has pointed out, they resemble those of a mine belonging to the industrial revolution. He has also noted a rather disturbing fact: 'several of the tunnels discovered below ground are tiny, and could only have been worked by children'.

We also have evidence for other Early Bronze Age copper mines in Wales. At Copa Hill near Aberystwyth copper mining began around 2100 BC and continued to c. 14000 BC. Although not as large as the mine at the Great Orme, a substantial opencast mine was nevertheless dug by the Bronze Age miners. Around 3500 cubic metres of rock spoil fill the opencast today, which points to the scale of activity during the Bronze Age.

During investigations at the mine in 1994, a hollowed out tree trunk was found preserved in waterlogged conditions. It is likely that the prehistoric miners used this tree trunk as a pipe to drain the mine when it became flooded. Hundreds of hammerstones were also found, with most showing abrasions, which reveal that they were hafted to handles of some sort.

At Nantyreira in mid Wales, there is firm evidence for Early Bronze mining activity, with hammerstones found in association with charcoal that gave radiocarbon dates of c. 1900-1600 BC. At Parys Mountain, Anglesey the evidence is inconclusive but suggests that an extensive Early Bronze Age mine once existed here. Early Bronze Age mines are also suspected at other mining sites in Wales (e.g. above Llŷn Llydaw and near Llanberis in Snowdonia) and future research will hopefully bring further mines of this period to light.

We have touched then upon the day to day lives of the people of the Early Bronze Age, but it is time now to turn to the more mysterious side of their existence and in the following chapter, we will examine the standing stones of the peninsula.

Chapter 5

# The Mystery of the Stones

'Enigmatic' is a word that is perhaps overused in prehistoric studies, but there seems no other one more apt to describe the standing stones of Llŷn, Arfon and Eifionydd. These impressive monoliths stand silent and alone in hidden corners of the peninsula and as Michael Senior rightly says in the *Standing Stones of north-western Wales*: 'cry out to be understood'. Although some scholars feel that this is beyond our reach, does this mean that we should not try to understand them?

After all, the study of prehistory is often an intellectual endeavour in which we strive to uncover the meaning of the past from mute, archaeological evidence. In this chapter then, the standing stones of the peninsula will be examined and the more plausible theories on standing stones discussed. Some of my own observations on the standing stones of the peninsula will also be put forward; though of course I do not claim to have uncovered the truth regarding these intriguing monuments. I hope that people will visit the stones of the peninsula themselves, make their own observations about them and gain as much pleasure as I have from being confronted with an ancient mystery.

### Dating Standing Stones
Although it is often hard to firmly date standing stones, it is apparent from the archaeological evidence that has been found, that many were erected during the Early Bronze Age c. 2500-1500 BC. It would be fair to assume that many of the standing stones of the peninsula were also erected during this period, though a word of warning should be made here. It is possible that some of the standing stones are boundary markers erected during the medieval period and some may even be unmarked gravestones, erected during the Early Christian period. Another possibility is that some of the standing stones (particularly the smaller examples) were set up as 'rubbing stones' for livestock. It has even been

reported that in the Saint Ishmaels area of Pembrokeshire, two neighbouring farmers engaged in a competition to see who could set up the largest rubbing stone!

Nevertheless, it does seem likely that a large number of the surviving standing stones of the peninsula do date to the Early Bronze Age and there is evidence from some standing stones in the peninsula, which indicates that they were erected during this period of prehistory. Before we begin our visit to the standing stones, we will take a look at some of the theories put forward regarding these mysterious monuments.

## Standing Stones as Route Markers

A number of scholars have suggested that prehistoric people erected standing stones in order to mark important routes across the landscape. Is it possible that some of the standing stones of Llŷn, Arfon and Eifionydd were erected for this purpose? While it may be the case that some standing stones are situated close to ancient routes across the peninsula, it seems somewhat unlikely that its prehistoric communities would have needed to mark the tracks that they used.

We have to remember that the people of this time lived close to nature and must have been very aware of their surrounding environment. It would surely have been easier for them to use familiar natural features such as hills, rivers and even trees and rocks as reference points in the landscape. In any case, the tracks themselves would have been obvious features in the landscape and standing stones 'advertising' their presence seem unnecessary.

The archaeological evidence found at standing stones suggests that they were monuments where ceremonies and rituals associated with religion took place. It is more probable that when they were situated near prehistoric tracks, it was in order to draw attention to their religious importance, rather than indicate the correct route through the landscape.

One possibility regarding standing stones placed by prehistoric trackways is that they were located in such places so as to 'guard' the living who passed along these routes across the landscape. Trevor Garnham has suggested that some of the standing stones on Orkney were imbued with a sacred power, which protected the living from 'the potentially malevolent sprits of the dead'. George Williams has also followed a similar line of reasoning in his study of the standing stones of Wales and south-west England and suggested that they represent 'aniconic representations of a supernatural being'.

## Astronomical Associations

Another theory that we have to take into account in our study of the standing stones of the peninsula is that they may have some connection with astronomical events. Although this is a contentious issue, it should not simply be dismissed out of hand. There is a considerable body of evidence from the British Isles, which reveals that prehistoric people aligned other ritual monuments on the movements of the sun and moon. It also seems likely that prehistoric people aligned some of their monuments on the stars, but we have no firm evidence for this. We will briefly consider some of the evidence for prehistoric solar and lunar alignments before the possibility that the standing stones of the peninsula had some astronomical purpose is examined.

Mention was made in chapter 2 of the alignment of the Newgrange tomb on the midwinter sunrise. A similar alignment has been noted at the impressive passage grave of Maes Howe on Orkney. At this late Neolithic tomb (c. 2700 BC), the passage which faced south-west, was aligned so that the light of the midwinter sunset penetrated into the dark recesses of the burial chamber. In Wales, recent research at the fine passage grave of Bryn Celli Ddu on Ynys Môn has revealed that its builders also incorporated an astronomical alignment into the tomb. This research, undertaken by Steve Burrow of the National Museum of Wales has shown that the passage at Bryn Celli Ddu is orientated on the midsummer sunrise.

Aubrey Burl, the renowned authority on prehistoric ritual and religion in the British Isles, has discovered that Cornish stone circles of the Late Neolithic/Early Bronze Age were orientated towards the early November sunset. To the pre-Christian Celts, early November marked the festival of Samhain (today's Halloween), when the New Year began and malignant spirits had to be driven from the land. The orientation of the Cornish stone circles perhaps indicates that Iron Age, Celtic rituals and beliefs had a long heritage stretching back at least as far as the Early Bronze Age.

However, it was not just the movements of the sun that played an integral part in the erection of many prehistoric monuments. Aubrey Burl has also noted in his study of the recumbent stone circles of Aberdeenshire, that these unusual monuments were aligned on the midsummer moon as it shone high in the southern sky.

It is also known that the first phase of construction at Stonehenge (the actual 'henge' which comprises of the bank and ditch which ring the stones – built around 3200 BC) incorporated not only a solar alignment on the midsummer sunrise, bur also probably a lunar one on the moon's major rising in the northern sky.

We have briefly seen then, some of the evidence pertaining to the astronomical alignments found at prehistoric monuments, but is there any evidence that the single standing stones of the Early Bronze Age were associated with astronomical events?

Unfortunately, it has to be admitted that when it comes to possible astronomical alignments at standing stones, we are straying into the realms of speculation. The main problem with standing stones in this respect is that as they often have two long sides or faces and also quite frequently, a sloping or pointed top. We are therefore faced with a number of choices when it comes to the part of the horizon that the stone 'points' towards, if it is pointing anywhere at all.

Nevertheless, although solar and lunar alignments at standing stones are questionable, considering the plentiful evidence for astronomical alignments at other prehistoric monuments, it seems probable that some standing stones were positioned in line with astronomical events. There does in fact appear to be some evidence for this practice in the British Isles and it will be worthwhile to take a brief look at this.

For example, at the site of Kintraw in Argyll, an early Bronze Age cairn is associated with a standing stone. In his book, *The Megalith Builders*, Euan Mackie proposes that the standing stone was aligned on a notch between the peaks of Beinn Shiantaidh and Beinn an Oir on the island of Jura some

45km away. Mackie feels that the standing stone was used as a solar observatory because around 1800 BC, the midwinter sun would have set in the notch between the above peaks.

John Wood in *Sun, Moon and Standing Stones* has also made claims for astronomical alignments at single standing stones in Scotland. For example, he claims that a standing stone at Ballinaby on the island of Islay in the Hebrides was in line with a notch on the horizon, so that the moon setting at its most northerly declination could be observed.

Alexander Thom, a highly skilled surveyor and mathematician who devoted a huge amount of time and energy to recording astronomical alignments at megalithic sites, also proposed that standing stones were used in astronomical alignments. Among other places, he surveyed isolated standing stones in Scotland and Brittany suggesting that they were used in both solar and lunar alignments.

As we shall see below, there may be indications that some standing stone of the peninsula were aligned on astronomical events. However, any suggestions I put forward in regard to this are tentative at best and this is an area of investigation that is perhaps worthy of more detailed study by someone skilled in such matters.

Why astronomical alignments were incorporated into prehistoric monuments is not exactly clear. It seems unlikely that they reveal the existence of astronomy as an objective science and that prehistoric people were conducting scientific research into the movements of the sun and moon. What does seem more probable is that they reveal unknown religious beliefs about these celestial bodies and that such alignments were symbolic in nature, rather than precisely worked out sightlines to celestial events. Also, the alignments at Neolithic tombs surely indicate a connection with ideas about death and rebirth. We are not looking then at prehistoric astronomers who were driven by intellectual curiosity but rather, people who were driven by such things as religious faith, fear and superstition.

It should also be mentioned that ethnographic studies from around the world have shown how many 'primitive' societies worshipped the sun and moon as powerful gods. It is also known that the worship of the sun and the moon was widespread amongst ancient civilisations such as the Aztecs, the Babylonians and the ancient Egyptians. Whilst not proving similar beliefs among our prehistoric forebears, such evidence does suggest their likelihood and it could be that some of the standing stones of the peninsula were erected because of similar beliefs.

## Sacred Peaks

While it is clear that prehistoric people aligned their monuments on solar and lunar events, it is likely that it was not always these events that concerned them. There is a fair amount of evidence from the British Isles, which strongly suggests that prehistoric monuments were also aligned on conspicuous hills and mountains. We can not say with certainty why this was, but as we have previously discussed in the chapter on the axe factory at Mynydd Rhiw, it probably relates to the prehistoric conception that such places were somehow connected to the otherworld.

It is likely that the headland of Mynydd Rhiw, marks only a small component of the 'sacred geography' of the peninsula during the Neolithic period and that other conspicuous hills and mountains were bound up with the religious beliefs of the people of this time. Likewise, the same is likely to have been true for the communities of the Early Bronze Age, who erected many of the peninsula's standing stones. Therefore, it does not seem unreasonable to suggest that some standing stones in the peninsula were sited in the landscape, in order to draw attention to parts of it that were considered to be sacred by these communities.

Insights into the 'primitive' worldview of prehistoric people regarding hills and mountains can again be provided by ethnographic studies. For example, in North America, the Black Hills mountain range on the northern plains was central to the religious beliefs of a number of native groups who lived in this area. Among the Cheyenne, Bear Butte was the most sacred mountain and was seen as a spirit lodge where the gods resided, while below them in the underground caverns lived the animal sprits. For the Lakota, the Black Hills were associated with the mythical hero 'Falling Star', who travelled through the 'Star Villages', while the Kiowa associated the peak known as the 'Devil's Tower' with myths about their hero-god, who was known as' Sun-Boy' or 'Half-Boy'.

Of course we cannot simply 'transplant' such belief systems onto prehistoric societies who lived thousands of years before the native inhabitants of North America. However, they do suggest that the former probably saw the landscape as a sacred place and that mountains and hills played a large part in the religious traditions of prehistoric times.

## Other Theories on the Stones

There have been other plausible suggestions put forward regarding the function of standing stones and we will examine some of these before proceeding to our study of the standing stones of the peninsula.

One interesting possibility is that standing stones were explicitly associated with the ancestors. It is known for instance, that among groups in the highlands of Madagascar, standing stones known as vatolahy stones ('man stones') have been erected since the 14th century. These are erected to celebrate a deceased individual who has won renown in life, or to honour an individual who has died and now resides in his ancestral tomb.

The living can ask for the help of the ancestral spirits at vatolahy stones and gifts are left at them if good luck follows these requests for spiritual intervention. Obviously cross-cultural generalisations such as this do not prove a similar function for standing stones of the Early Bronze Age, but they perhaps help to bring us closer to the beliefs of our prehistoric ancestors.

Other possible functions for standing stones are that they were meeting places, marked territories and boundaries (both real and sacred), or commemorated important events such as the inauguration of a chief, or the winning or losing of a battle. We do know that burials were associated with some standing stones (as we shall see below, there is an example of this in the peninsula), although whether such stones were set up primarily as grave markers is unknown – though it does perhaps seem probable.

Of course the functions of standing stones may not have been exclusive of one another. For example, a standing stone may have been the focus of ancestor worship, and an integral part of this worship may also have been the stone's alignment on the sun or moon and a sacred part of the landscape. As Michael Senior has said: 'one of the things we may have to do, looking at the standing stones, is to resist our wish to see them in terms of fixed and direct purpose'.

## The Standing Stones of Llŷn, Arfon and Eifionydd

The standing stones of the peninsula come in various shapes and sizes, but we can perhaps classify them into three 'types'. There are tall, narrow stones, which are rather elegant and rectangular in section and tall stones which are also finely shaped and rectangular in section, but broader in width. There are also the standing stones that can perhaps best be described as 'wedge-shaped' and these seem to be the dominant type. Finally, it should be pointed out that there are some standing stones that cannot really be included in any of the above groups because of their unusual shape.

Although it is hard to say for sure, it is probable that some standing stones of the peninsula were shaped or 'dressed' with stone tools after they had been prised from the ground while other stones were simply raised as they had been found. The different shapes and heights of the standing stones in the peninsula may suggest that different groups had different traditions when it came to raising these monuments in the landscape. Also, several of the stones also appear to have pointed or sloping tops, as is often the case with standing stones elsewhere, though exactly what this means is hard to say.

### Sarn Mellteyrn *(15)*

This tall and elegant stone is some 8 ft in height and is one of the most impressive standing stones in the whole of the peninsula. It is situated in a picturesque and peaceful spot (as with many of the peninsula's standing stones) in Saint Peter's churchyard outside Sarn Mellteyrn. Like the Neolithic tomb at Mynydd Cefn Amwlch (which lies some 2 miles to the north-west) it is located above a valley through which the Afon Soch runs and lies close to a route inland from the west coast of Llŷn.

Although this standing stone could be a memorial stone dating to the early Christian period, this is unlikely as the holes apparent in its face reveal how a lantern was hung here in former times. It is improbable that an Early Christian monument would have been treated with such a lack of respect and it is more likely that the stone is prehistoric and that it was 'christianised' by its incorporation into the churchyard. Similar prehistoric standing stones can be found in several other churchyards throughout Wales and reveal the efforts of the Early Christians to turn the people away from deeply entrenched pagan religious beliefs and practices that originated in the country's prehistoric past.

What is apparent when visiting this stone, is that your attention is directed towards Garn Fadrun to the north-east and one of faces of the stone is directed towards the mountain. However, there is some uncertainty as to whether the stone stands in its original position and it is possible that the stone has been reset in the recent past and therefore, this 'alignment' may simply be fortuitous. Nevertheless, it seems unlikely that the stone has been moved any great distance from the position it may have occupied in the Early Bronze Age and so, it would still have looked out over the river valley towards Garn Fadrun.

### Llangwnnadl (16)

This standing stone lies near the end of the peninsula on the western coast of Llŷn and is situated about 3 miles to the west of the above monument and is similar in appearance, though somewhat taller at around 10 ft. The proximity of the stones and their similarity (although the Llangwnnadl stone has a broken top), perhaps indicates that they were erected by the same group who occupied this corner of Llŷn. Another aspect of this stone that perhaps lends further support to this idea is that like its counterpart at St Peter's, it also has one of its faces directed towards Garn Fadrun, which can be seen to the north-east. However, as we have seen above, there is some uncertainty over the original position of the standing stone in the churchyard.

### Pandy Saethon (16a)

This stone is perhaps the strongest candidate for the astronomical marker theory, and although as mentioned above I am not claiming to have uncovered the truth, this stone may warrant further investigation in this respect. It is extremely doubtful that standing stones were arbitrarily placed in the landscape and the location of this monument strongly suggests that views of the horizon and sky were important factors in the choice of its location.

This fairly modest, unusually shaped stone (it is almost needle-like in its appearance and c. 5.5 ft in height) stands above the valley of the Afon Horon and is situated on a plateau above its wooded slopes. From the stone, there are fine views south-west towards the headland of Mynydd Rhiw and Mynydd Cilan and the sweep of Porth Neigwl can also be seen to the south. There may be some astronomical 'connection' between the stone and Mynydd Rhiw as the stone does provide a very good location from which to watch the sun setting behind the headland, but beyond this I cannot say more. Perhaps of even greater significance, is that as you look north-west the top of the stone appears to be in line with a noticeable gap between the peaks of Garn Fadrun and Garn Bach, though this could be simply down to chance rather than intention.

We should perhaps also bear in mind that Mynydd Rhiw seems to have been a sacred part of the landscape in the prehistoric period and mention has already been made in chapter 3 of the various prehistoric ritual and ceremonial monuments on Mynydd Rhiw that seem to attest to this. Another possibility therefore, is that the Pandy Saethon stone was erected by people of the Early Bronze Age in order to 'honour' a part of the landscape that was part of the 'sacred geography' of the peninsula.

### Nant y Gledrydd *(17)*

This impressive standing stone measures around 7.5 ft. and is located on the lower slopes of Garn Fadrun, which can be seen to south-west, while to the north-east the upper slopes of Garn Boduan can also be seen. There may be some astronomical relationship between Garn Fadrun and this monument because as Michael Senior has pointed out, the top of the stone seems to be in line with a notch in Garn Fadrun's outline. However, as with the stone at Pandy Saethon the orientation of the standing stone on this notch could be simply down to chance. It is perhaps worth noting though, that the monument is located in a position that gives a clear view of Garn Fadrun between two wooded ridges.

## Yr Eifl (17a)

This standing stone lies very close to the footpath that leads to Tre'r Ceiri and Yr Eifl and the pass that runs below these peaks to Llanaelhaearn and then onwards towards Clynnog. It seems highly likely that the modern footpath follows the course of a long-lived track that would also have been used in the prehistoric period and so the stone may have been set up here in order to attract the attention of prehistoric travellers.

Also of possible interest is the fact that the burial cairn on Mynydd Carnguwch is immediately apparent from the stone and the south-western summit of Yr Eifl – on which burial cairns of the Early Bronze Age are also located. It is possible that therefore, that the Yr Eifl stone was 'referencing' sacred parts of the landscape. The stone also offers superb views across the peninsula and to the south-east the mountains of Snowdonia and Mid Wales can be seen, while to the south-west, the countryside of Llŷn opens out before you. However, we should also bear in mind that this stone may have been set up in more recent times and had some other function, such as a rubbing stone for animals.

## The Tir-Gwyn stones (18, 19)

These two standing stones one about 200 yards apart in a field near the small but distinctive hill known as Moelypenmaen. The larger of the stones is very impressive and stands at around 10ft high. It also has a somewhat crooked appearance, as the top of the stone kinks towards the east. The smaller of the two stones is about 6 ft in height and like its counterpart tapers towards the top.

A number of finds were made near the stones and consist of a flint flake and a 'plano-convex', flint knife. These finds indicate that prehistoric people came to the stones and may represent evidence of religious ceremonies taking place here – or they were simply left behind by the workforce that erected the stones. Two burials from the early Christian period (which will be discussed later) were also found in the field between the two stones, though it is very unlikely that the stones were raised as memorial stones to the deceased as similar pairs of prehistoric stones are known from elsewhere in Wales. It is possible that the burials were placed here in order to christianise a pagan site, but it is also possible that Early Christians were drawn to the stones because they found it hard to let go of beliefs that had their roots in the prehistoric period.

The stones are situated in an impressive location and are surrounded by a series of hills and mountains that run in an arc from south-west to north-east. At the south-western end of this arc is Moelypenmaen and Garn Boduan, while its north-eastern end is a marked by Yr Eifl and the distinctive, dome-shaped hill known as Mynydd Carnguwch. The huge, Early Bronze Age burial cairn can also be easily seen on the summit of Mynydd Carnguwch and as with the Pandy Saethon stone the relationship between the stones and the land and sky is striking. The close proximity of Moelypenmaen to the stones may also be of some significance.

Again without further detailed investigation, it is hard to say whether any astronomical alignments exist, though we can probably exclude one on the axis of the stones, which runs almost due north to south. These are areas of the sky where the sun and moon do not appear, though this of course does not disprove an alignment on the axis of the stones, as there could be a number of unknown reasons for this alignment, if it was indeed intentional.

### Trallwyn *(20)*

This impressive monument, which measures about 8ft high is located near Mynydd Carnguwch and provides us with a fascinating conundrum. As mentioned above, the summit of Mynydd Carnguwch is crowned by a huge burial cairn of the Early Bronze Age, which will be discussed in more detail in the next chapter. This cairn can easily be seen from the standing stone, but the intriguing question is whether there is any relationship between the two monuments?

The location of the standing stone strongly suggests that its primary purpose was to draw attention to the burial cairn and it may have been a location where ceremonies and rituals connected with the ancestors were performed. The top of the stone does appear to 'point' to the cairn on the top of Mynydd Carnguwch and although this of course could be fortuitous, it is hard to escape the feeling that there is some connection between the two monuments. Unfortunately however, without excavation we cannot say whether the two monuments are 'contemporary', or whether the standing stone was erected before (or even a long time after) the building of the cairn.

### Cefngraenog (21)
With its long rectangular profile, this impressive monument is the most regularly shaped of the peninsula's standing stones, and it is likely that this shape was achieved by some dressing of the stone. The stone is situated on a ridge and this location coupled with its height (c.10 ft.) means that it can easily be seen when approaching from a distance.

Like its counterpart at Trallwyn, the exact relationship between this standing stone and the remains of burial cairns that lie nearby is unclear. It is possible that that the monuments are not contemporary and that the standing stone post-dates the cairns, though the stone could have been erected at the same time as the cairns (which may date to the Middle Bronze Age, c. 1300 BC). Alternatively, this fine standing stone could have been here many hundreds of years before the burial mounds were built and the Bronze Age people who buried their dead in these cairns could have been attracted to this location because of the ancient and scared standing stone, which was associated with the ancestors.

### Glynllifon (22)
We are again presented with another puzzle when it comes to this fine monument, which is perhaps the most impressive standing stone in the peninsula and it has an indefinable air about it that is suggestive of strength and authority. Whether it is oriented on any landscape feature is hard to say, but looking eastwards the top of Mynydd y Cilgwyn can be seen in the distance. The stone stands near one of the entrances to Glynllifon Country Park and measures around 9.5 ft in height. In 1875, an excavation was undertaken by F.G. Wynn near the stone and he discovered calcined bone, charcoal and

fragments of a burial urn of the Early Bronze Age (probably a 'Food Vessel' dating to c. 2000-1500 BC)

The question however, is of the relationship between the standing stone and the excavated material found near it. Does this suggest that the standing stone was erected as a memorial to an important individual and thus functioned as a grave marker? Alternatively, did the deceased choose to be buried by the stone because they wished to be associated with it for some reason that is lost to us? Unfortunately this is a question that can probably never be answered.

### Betws Fawr (23)

This monument is similar in appearance to the stone at Cefngraeanog (though is a little smaller at 8 ft high) and stands in splendid isolation in a field near the Afon Dwyfach. From the stone there are extensive views east towards the mountains of Snowdonia, while to the north and west the mountains and hills of the peninsula can be seen. When visiting this monument you are struck by a similar feeling to the one experienced at the Pandy Saethon and Tir Gwyn stones – that wide horizons and the sky were important in the location of the stone.

It is known that another standing stone once stood nearby but was removed by a local farmer. Shortly afterwards several of his cattle suddenly died and it is said that his neighbours felt that this was deserved because of his sacrilegious act of removing the stone. Such stories are abundant in Welsh folklore, but the attitude of the unfortunate farmer's neighbours perhaps preserves the remnants of more ancient beliefs.

### Tyddyn Mawr (24)

This standing stone (c.6 ft in height) could represent all that remains of a stone circle that once stood in the bare and lonely uplands near the neck of the peninsula. It is listed as a stone circle in the megalithic monument inventory that appears in the *Atlas of Caernarfonshire* (published by Gwynedd Rural Council in 1977). This may well be a correct classification as the location of the stone in a sparsely populated upland region, conforms to a pattern recognised at other stone circles in Wales. Lying close to the stone (some

50m to the west) is a distinctive, flat-topped large outcrop of rock, which as suggested by Gwynedd Archaeological Trust, may well have been used in religious ceremonies and rituals connected with the standing stone/stone circle. This standing stone is well worth a visit as there are stunning views to be had from the monument (as there are with many of the peninsula's standing stones).

### Tir-Bach *(25, 26)*

In comparison to most other standing stones in the peninsula, this monument sits in an unusual location but there is however, some question over its prehistoric authenticity. The stone stands at around 6 ft high and although wedge-shaped it has an unusual symmetry about it, which gives it an almost arrow-like appearance.

The question of its authenticity arises because of the carved graffiti that the stone has on both its upper and lower parts (although this is now hard to see because of weathering). On the lower part of the stone 1853 can be seen upside down, while on the upper part can be seen 1866 the right way up. This suggests perhaps that the stone was reset between these dates, with the present top of the stone having been below ground. This however seems rather unlikely, as the stone would have been very unstable – whether erected by prehistoric or modern people. The present cottage at Tir-Bach was built in 1853 and so the stone may have been erected on the occasion of its completion. I feel it is more probable however, that the earlier graffiti on the stone was made when it was lying recumbent and that the later made when it was reset. For me, the clues to the prehistoric authenticity of this stone lie in the surrounding landscape, though of course this may simply be wishful thinking on my part!

Firstly, the stone stands in flat marshy ground very close to the Afon Erch, which runs past it on its western side and the river's close proximity to the stone could have something to do with its location. We have already discussed the prehistoric veneration of water and we should take this into account when we come to consider the significance of this standing stone's location.

Also of interest is the fact that the stone sits in a natural bowl or 'amphitheatre' and has no views outside of this. It is enclosed, hidden almost, and one gets a feeling at this stone that it was placed in this dell so that your attention is focused on the immediate surroundings. This is in contrast to the other standing stones of the peninsula, which seem to direct attention away from themselves to various points in the wider landscape. What this indicates is unclear, but perhaps it is possible that the stone was erected here by a prehistoric community because this secluded dell with a sacred river running through it, was considered to be a special part of the landscape?

### Capel Tan y Foel (27)

This finely shaped standing stone, which is about 6ft in height, is located in a field wall that runs alongside the lane leading from the old chapel of Tan y Foel, on Mynydd Rhiw. It is situated in a location that has fine views south-west towards the peninsula's end and Ynys Enlli can clearly be seen from the standing stone. The fact that the view towards the north and east is blocked by rising ground may indicate that your view is being directed intentionally to the south-west.

### Bodfan (28, 29)

This is perhaps the most unusual standing stone of the peninsula because it has such an odd appearance The stone although small (c. 5 ft) is powerfully squat and looks almost as though it has twisted itself as it has erupted from the ground. It is located in farmland close to Dinas Dinlle and the peaks that mark the entrance to Llŷn can be seen to the south-west. Like other standing stones in the peninsula it is located in a position that allows wide views of the land and sky and it is possible that there is some connection between the stone and the peaks of Yr Eifl, which are particularly noticeable on the south-western horizon.

### Llyn Glasfryn (30, 31, 32, 32a)

I did not discover this pair of standing stones until 2005 when I was doing further research for this book. Like the stones at Tir Gwyn, we seem to have an example of an alignment, though again it is hard to be sure on what the Glasfryn stones are aligned – if anything. The stones stand at the end of a lake known as Llyn Glasfryn (which is found on the country estate of the same name) and are located in what has to be one of the most beautiful corners of the peninsula. The standing stone found on a hillock at the south-western end of the lake has to rank among the finest in the peninsula and stands at c. 11ft tall. This monument which is made from a narrow stone slab has a blade-like appearance, which is further accentuated by its sharp pointed top which may have been broken at some point?

The other, much smaller standing stone (c.5ft) is located about 350 yards to the north-west, in a field in front of the splendid country house at Glasfryn and Tre'r Ceiri can be seen rising behind the house in the distance. It is possible that the axis of the alignment points towards this prominent peak either because of some astronomical or sacred connection. However, if you stand with your back against the larger of the stones its flat face is directed west towards a noticeable gap between Mynydd Nefyn and Gwylwyr Carreglefain, which may indicate that something of astronomical significance occurs on this part of the horizon. Another possibility that is also worthy of consideration is that there is some connection between the standing stones and nearby Llyn Glasfryn. It has been mentioned previously, that water seems to have been seen as sacred by prehistoric people and that the stone at Tir Bach may have been located near a river that was revered by an Early Bronze Age community that lived in this area. Likewise, the Glasfryn stones may have been located close to the lake because they were 'honouring' a special area of the landscape that was connected with the spirit world. What is perhaps interesting in this respect is that the larger of the two stones seems to have been deliberately positioned on higher ground at the north-eastern end of the lake, so that it looks out over it. It is perhaps also worth mentioning that Ffynnon Grasi holy well lies nearby at the eastern end of the lake, which may indicate that early Christians came to a pagan site and christianised it by converting a well that may also have been revered by prehistoric people.

What is also intriguing about both the Tir Gwyn and Glasfryn stones, is the fact that in both 'alignments' one standing stone is much smaller than the other and the stones not only show a discrepancy in size, but also in shape. A similar situation has been noted in west Wales where there are many pairs of standing stones and C.J. Dunn has suggested that the pairing of standing stones may be 'related to the symbolic deification of male and female and their attributes'. This theory may be impossible to prove, but it is a thought-provoking one nevertheless.

Finally, it should be pointed out that as these stones are not marked on the OS map and I have found no reference to them in the literature, there is a possibility that they were raised in more recent times. However their size, location and appearance does seem to suggest otherwise.

### Gyrn Ddu *(33, 34)*

As with the above monument at Tir-Bach there is some doubt over the prehistoric authenticity of this stone, though there are several aspects of its appearance which may suggest that was set up during the Early Bronze Age.

The stone is set into the end of a field wall that surrounds a deserted farmhouse, which lies at the foot of Gyrn Ddu and Moel Bronmiod. However it seems unlikely that it functioned as gatepost as it features no holes for the attachment of one and it is also quite large (about 7ft high) and irregular in appearance, which gives it a prehistoric 'feel'. Also it lies close to a footpath that probably follows a prehistoric route, which led through the uplands of Arfon to passes that led to the coast near Clynnog Fawr and inland to the eastern edge of the peninsula.

The final thing which may be of some significance as regards to a postulated prehistoric date for the stone, is that there is a fine view of the burial cairn on Mynydd Carnguwch from it and one of its faces does 'point' towards this peak. It is possible therefore that this standing stone was similar to the monument at Trallwyn, which seems to almost act as 'sign-post' for the burial cairn on Mynydd Carnguwch.

### Morfa Abererch *(35)*

In terms of location, this has to be the most unusual standing stone in the whole of the peninsula as it is located on the edge of the long and curving beach that runs from Pwllheli to Penychain. The stone stands on a low promontory, which juts out from the sand dunes and although it is now partly covered by sand, the stone appears to have stood about 5 ft high originally.

It is apparent that the stone has been deliberately set up and although it is hard to say for sure when it was erected, Gwynedd Archaeological Trust feel that it is more than likely prehistoric in date. Why prehistoric people chose to erect a stone on the edge of this beach will remain a mystery, but it may well have marked a burial place. As the Trust have noted, it would be worthwhile investigating the area around the stone as continued erosion poses a threat to any burial/s that may have been made close to the stone in prehistoric times.

## Glan Afon (36)

This narrow, slab-like stone is located not far from the above monument (about 1.5 miles) on the outskirts of Pwllheli. Although it is not marked on the Ordnance Survey map of the peninsula and its date is uncertain, its size (c. 7ft in height) suggests that it was not set up in more recent times as a rubbing stone for livestock. It is possible therefore, that it was erected by a prehistoric community of the Early Bronze Age and originally had some sort of religious function.

In terms of location, this standing stone is similar to the one foud at Tir Bach, as it also stands close to the Afon Erch (though not as close as the former monument) and is located in a somewhat enclosed landscape that does not offer wide-ranging views. However, in part, this is due to the sand dunes that lie nearby to the south of the stone and these may not have been here when the stone was raised in the Early Bronze Age (if it does indeed date to this period).

## Plas ym Mhenllech (37)

As mentioned in Chapter 2, this standing stone once featured carved cupmarks, but unfortunately these appear to have weathered away – although an expert may still be able discern traces of them? The stone is not particularly large and stands at around 3.5 ft high, though it is fairly broad and somewhat squat in appearance. Also mentioned in Chapter 2 was the possibility that this stone originated from the Mynydd Cefnamwlch Neolithic tomb, though we shall never know whether this theory is true.

## Chapter 6

# The Beaker People? In the Peninsula

### Beakers, Beer and Bowmen

Mention was made in chapter 4 of how the traditional view of the Beaker people is likely to have been wrongly dismissed by many archaeologists in recent years. This view reflects a general 'backlash' by modern archaeologists against the idea that new ways of life were brought into the British Isles during the prehistoric period by immigrants from abroad. Thus other significant prehistoric periods in the British Isles – such as the Neolithic or Iron Age – were not initiated by newcomers from the continent but by such things as the exchange of prestige goods between leaders of distant communities. Whatever the reality regarding the Neolithic or Iron Age, as will subsequently be seen, recent archaeological discoveries strongly suggest that the current trend in archaeological thinking regarding the Beaker people is questionable. These discoveries will be examined below, along with the evidence for the Beaker people in the peninsula. Firstly though, archaeological evidence found in other Beaker burials in the British Isles will be discussed to see what it may reveal about Beaker society.

The most instantly recognisable artefacts of Beaker burials are the distinctive Beakers, which accompanied the deceased. Beaker pottery is often well made and elaborately decorated with intricate designs and some beakers such as the 'Wessex/Middle Rhine' beakers were of an exceptional quality. These pots have a striking red finish, which is similar to that of the famous Roman Samian ware, and they must have been highly impressive objects that would have been greatly admired by the people who first set eyes on them. The various impressed designs found on Beakers were made in a number of ways. The earliest AOC (All-Over-Corded) beakers were decorated by twisting cord around the wet clay, which was then burned away during the firing of the pot, while many later beakers were decorated with bone or wooden combs. Fingernails were also used to make the designs found on beakers and other implements such as bone points and sharpened sticks must also have been used

The fineness of the beakers taken together with their inclusion in burials indicates that they had a special role amongst the communities of this time and there is archaeological evidence which strongly suggests that they were used to hold alcohol. At Ashgrove near Fife, careful analysis of a Beaker grave revealed that the beaker found in it had once held a type of mead that had been made from fermented lime flowers and had probably been flavoured with meadowsweet, heather and ribwort.

Another possibility is that beakers contained a mind-altering substance that was used in rituals and ceremonies connected with the spirit world (of course, alcohol can also be classed as a mind altering drug!). In this respect, Aubrey Burl has put forward the intriguing theory that beakers may have been used as drinking vessels that contained the urine of people who had eaten Fly Agaric (*Amanita muscaria*) toadstools, which are common to many parts of the British Isles. Although highly poisonous, Fly Agaric toadstools can produce strong, hallucinatory experiences if ingested in moderation and Burl has pointed out that documented examples exists of people drinking the urine of 'intoxicated priests' who had eaten *A. muscaria*. Some archaeologists have also proposed the idea that the cord used to decorate many beakers was actually cannabis hemp – suggesting perhaps that it was mixed with the alcoholic contents of the beakers to produce a potent drink. Although, the idea that the 'Beaker Folk' were cannabis users is probably a little fanciful (though not impossible), the idea that Beakers could contain hallucinogens perhaps carries more weight. It is more likely however, that they were used mainly as vessels to hold an early form of beer.

Another characteristic feature of beaker burials is the archers' equipment that was placed with the dead. This equipment consists of finely made flint 'barbed and tanged' arrowheads and 'bracers' of stone clay or bone, which were very probably used to protect archers' wrists from the lash of bowstrings (similar wristguards are still used by modern archers). It is evident that in some cases, arrowheads were made solely for use in the world of the dead and their fineness shows that they were 'ceremonial' in character. For example, at Breach Farm in Glamorgan, the 13 barbed and tanged arrowheads found in a Beaker barrow, were so thin and fragile that they can have had no practical use and must have been made solely as grave goods. Those arrowheads used in daily life would have been quite deadly and the barbs either side of the tang where the arrowshaft was attached would have helped to keep the arrow in the animal (or person) into which it had been fired.

Some of the bracers are of a high quality and two notable examples come from Beaker burials at Culduthal Mains (Inverness-shire) and Barnack (Cambridgeshire). These bracers are made from fine quality green schist and both feature gold caps on their ends. There is even an example of a bracer made from pure gold, which was found at Agua Branca in Portugal. This has led Joan Taylor to make the intriguing and plausible suggestion that there was a ranked Beaker 'archer class' and that gold was used as a means of denoting those archers who were at the top of this élite.

The bracer illustrated below comes from the famous burial at Stonehenge which was discovered by archaeologists in 1978. It was found with the skeleton of a man aged 25-30 years who had been buried in a crude pit in the ditch that surrounded the monument and it was evident that he had met a violent end. Three broken barbed and tanged arrowheads were found next to him and when the skeleton was later cleaned, the tips of these arrowheads were found embedded in his ribs and it appears that one had penetrated his heart. Why he was killed is a real puzzle but it is highly improbable that he was killed in an accident as the arrows had been fired at him from close range. One possibility is that he was a great warrior who was killed in battle and was accorded great honour by being buried at Stonehenge. Alternatively he may have been sacrificed to unknown gods or executed for some serious transgression. We will never know the answer to this ancient murder mystery, but we do know that the Stonehenge Archer was killed in the beaker period (c. 2500-2000 BC) as a radiocarbon date obtained from surviving tissue on the skeleton gave a date of c. 2200 BC for the man's death.

While the bracers and arrowheads found in Beaker burials reveal that archery was important to the people of this time, unfortunately no examples of Beaker bows have yet been found. However, tantalising traces of Beaker bows have been found in some burials. At Thwing in Yorkshire, a likely male burial (the body was oriented to the east which was common for men in Yorkshire Beaker burials) was discovered in a Beaker barrow and the fingers of the left hand were closed around a much decayed, unidentifiable item. Whether it represented the remains of a bow is open to question, but it had been made of wood. About 20 miles away at Callis Wold, the Yorkshire antiquarian, John Mortimer, excavated a round barrow in 1864. No burial was discovered in the barrow but five arrowheads and a curved streak of dark earth about three feet in length were found. Interestingly, in continental Beaker burials, tiny pendants that look very much like 'composite' bows have been found. These short and powerful bows are about a half the length of a longbow (about 6ft) and are known to have been used by ancient societies such as the Assyrians of ancient Iraq or the Scythians who lived on the Eurasian Steppes in the first millennium BC.

It may be that Beaker bowmen rode on horses that had been introduced into the British Isles by the Beaker people, but although horse bones are found on a number of Beaker sites in Europe it is perhaps somewhat difficult to reconcile the evidence with the idea. The bones of the horses reveal that they would have been about the same size as Exmoor ponies (about 4.5 feet high) and as yet, no piece of riding equipment has been found. Nevertheless, as Aubrey Burl has noted, the mustangs ridden by the native American Comanches were only a little bigger and Beaker riding gear, if it existed, would have been made from perishable materials such as leather.

As mentioned in chapter 4, the appearance of novel metal artefacts in Beaker graves led earlier archaeologists to the conclusion that it was continental Beaker immigrants who brought the knowledge of metalworking to the British Isles.

Small copper daggers have been recovered from a number of Beaker graves and while their value may have been largely symbolic rather than practical, they were still probably used as tools and weapons. They are known as 'tanged' daggers on account of the tang at the top of the blade, which was used for attaching a bone or wooden hilt and like Beaker pots are characteristically found in Beaker graves.

Also found in Beaker burials are the items of sheet gold such as the discs that were stitched onto clothing to be worn like a badge and the small, basket-shaped objects that are more than likely, earrings. That the gold discs were worn on clothing is revealed by the small perforations, which can still be seen in the middle and around their outer edges. These delicate objects which were probably of Irish origin (with the gold coming from the Wicklow Mountains), feature embossed circular patterns with a central cross or the 'cross-within-the-wheel' motif, but what they symbolise is unclear. It could be that they have some connection with sun worship, which has long been a suspected feature of Beaker religion and is known in many other ancient societies. Joan Taylor has put forward the interesting theory that these discs may have been worn by the leaders of Beaker 'prospecting' groups whose task it was to find copper, tin and gold in south-western Ireland. In support of her theory Dr Taylor points out that a concentration of these discs has been found near the Early Bronze Age mines at Mount Gabriel and Ballyvourney. Whatever the truth behind the discs, it is clear that persons of status wore them, as only a privileged few would have access to gold in Beaker society.

There are also some Beaker graves that appear to contain the burials of craftsmen. For example, in a well known Beaker burial close to the River Nene at Irthlingborough (Northants.), a male was accompanied by a range of artefacts which included a worked flint point, nine flint flakes, three bone spatulae (made from animal ribs) and a boar's tusk. It has been suggested that such items could have been used in the production of leather garments, which some archaeologists suggest were worn by Beaker people. Some Beaker graves also appear to contain the burials of metalworkers. In a barrow near Stonehenge, along with a fine Beaker, a highly polished, small rectangular stone (made from siliceous 'hornstone') was discovered. Similar stones are also known from continental Beaker graves and they have been interpreted as small anvils or 'cushion stones' that were used for working copper and gold.

Finally, before we look at the true nature of the 'Beaker Folk', mention has to be made of a very curious practice performed by the people of this time. This was the practice of 'trephination', which involved cutting a circular roundel of bone from a person's skull, presumably with a flint knife. It appears that trephination was not uncommon in the Beaker period and evidence of this practice has been found in the British Isles and Europe. For example, at Crichel Down in Dorset, a skull discovered in a Beaker burial had a large, circular opening cut into it and the cranial disc which had been removed to make the opening lay alongside it. In a Beaker burial at the Snail Down barrow cemetery near Stonehenge, a bone disc was found next to a cremation burial. Such examples provide evidence that in many cases this prehistoric brain surgery failed, but it could often be successful too. In Denmark, an individual had undergone three trepannings, before finally succumbing during the fourth operation. Why trephination – which must have caused tremendous pain and shock – was carried out is something of a mystery, but it may be that it was thought to cure such things as madness, epilepsy and migraines, which people attributed to evil spirits. It is even possible perhaps, that the alcohol, which the beakers probably contained, was used as a 'numbing agent' in some trepanning operations. Trephination was also carried out during the Neolithic, though it does not appear to have been a common practice and several examples of skulls from Iron Age contexts also display the characteristic holes from this operation.

### The Beaker 'People' – Myth or Reality?
The evidence from the Beaker burials reveals that in the Early Bronze Age there was a distinct change from the burial rite of the preceding Neolithic period, with collective burial in megalithic tombs and long barrows replaced by the dominant practice of individual burial under a round

mound. Traditionally this marked shift in the burial rite has been seen as the strongest evidence for the arrival of Beaker people from the continent. In the Neolithic tombs, grave goods were few and emphasis was on the anonymous group with the bones of the dead mixed together (although it is likely that these groups represent a privileged class in Neolithic society). In contrast, Beaker burials seem to honour important individuals whose status and role in society was indicated by their burial with grave goods in a round mound or flat grave.

Admittedly, it would be too simplistic to argue that that a change in burial practices equates with the arrival of a new people and in fact, at the end of the Neolithic, some individuals accompanied by grave goods were interred under barrows. This burial rite is most notable in the Yorkshire Wolds and in some cases, these barrows were huge (e.g. Duggleby Howe and Willie Howe). Therefore, those who refute the traditional idea of the Beaker people feel that Beaker burials point to an indigenous development derived from Late Neolithic burial practices, rather than evidence of the arrival of a new people in the British Isles during the final Neolithic.

However, as Neil Brodie has pointed out there may be a flaw in this theory of indigenous development for Beaker burials. In his thesis, *The Neolithic – Bronze Age Transition* in Britain he argues that in the final stage of the Neolithic in the British Isles, there was actually a discontinuity in burial practices. Brodie claims that the dominant burial rite that immediately preceded Beaker burials was disposal of the dead in cremation cemeteries (that were largely lacking in grave goods) and not individual burial under a barrow. Thus there may have actually have been an inversion in the burial practices of the final Neolithic rather than a progression to the widespread Beaker burials of the Early Bronze Age. While Brodie's argument is persuasive, like many archaeological theories it is open to question and not all would agree with it. So is there any firmer evidence that provides support for those who favour the 'traditional' view that Beaker burials reveal the existence in the British Isles of a dynamic people who arrived from the continent at the end of the Neolithic, bringing with them new ways of life and death? As will be seen below, the answer to this question appears to be 'yes'.

**The Amesbury Archer**
One of the most important and spectacular finds in British archaeology was made in May 2002 as Wessex Archaeology were excavating in advance of the building of a school at Boscombe Down, near Amesbury in Wiltshire. They discovered a Beaker grave that contained the complete skeleton of a man aged between thirty-five and forty-five years who had probably been buried in a timber chamber. There were no signs of a barrow covering the grave, but this could have been ploughed out by later farming.

The man was accompanied into the next life with the richest array of goods yet found in a Beaker grave in the British Isles and almost 100 artefacts were discovered in his grave. Although there were many flint tools and flakes, there was an unparalleled number of artefacts that are characteristic of Beaker burials. Included amongst the superb array of grave goods were five unusual Beakers, three copper daggers, two stone bracers, sixteen barbed and tanged arrowheads, four boar tusks, a shale ring, many flint flakes and tools, a cushion-stone and two basket-shaped, earrings or hair tresses. The large amount of archery equipment found in the man's grave led to the press dubbing him the 'Amesbury Archer', though he was also called 'King of Stonehenge' for reasons which will be explained below.

However, as fine as the grave of the Amesbury Archer was, the most significant aspect of the burial was discovered when his skeleton was scientifically studied, which included isotope analysis on the enamel of the archer's teeth. Basically, oxygen and strontium isotopes are trapped in teeth as a result of drinking water and provide a chemical 'fingerprint' that helps to determine a person's place of origin and obviously, this is very useful when studying ancient burials. The analysis revealed that the Amesbury Archer had been born in central Europe in the Alps, with his most likely place of origin being Switzerland. This was of huge importance because it appears to confirm that the Beaker people actually existed and that they originated on the continent and settled in the British Isles during the beginning of the Early Bronze Age.

Unexpectedly, another Beaker grave containing the skeleton of man aged about 25 was found close to the Archer's and analysis of both skeletons revealed the same, unusual bone structures in their feet. While it is probable that this skeletal evidence indicate that the younger man was the Archer's son, it does not prove this beyond doubt. Nevertheless, the two men were certainly closely related. It is also interesting to note that scientific analysis of the younger mans teeth revealed that he had lived in the Midlands or north-east Scotland as a teenager, though he could still have been born on the continent.

Other evidence which provides strong support for those who favour the traditional idea of the Beaker people comes from the Early Bronze Age copper mine at Ross Island in County Kerry. This unique site is the earliest copper mine yet known in Britain or Ireland (2400-2200 BC – placing it firmly in the Beaker period) and as noted previously, the first metal objects seen in the British Isles appear to have been produced in Ireland. Interestingly, large number of Beaker sherds were found at the site and it is apparent that the miners were deliberately targeting arsenic-rich copper ores, which was a feature of continental metalworking. The evidence therefore strongly suggests that the first metalworkers in Britain and Ireland were Beaker people from the continent

As mentioned previously, the Amesbury Archer has also been called 'King of Stonehenge'. This is because his rich burial, which lies about 2.5 miles from Stonehenge has been dated to c. 2300 BC (by analysis of the grave goods and radiocarbon dating), which is around the time that the huge stone circles at Stonehenge were erected. There is no doubt that the Amesbury Archer was a man of very high status in the Stonehenge region and is likely to have witnessed the replacement of the Neolithic timber monument with the huge stones that are so instantly recognisable today. Whether he was involved in its construction is open to question but as we have seen with the Stonehenge Archer, there does seem to be some connection between the Beaker people and

Stonhenge. In fact, before we move on to look at the Beaker burials of the peninsula it will be worthwhile looking at the evidence that Beaker groups from Wales could well have raised the first stones at Stonehenge.

### The Stonehenge 'Bluestones'

The building of Stonehenge was begun in the Late Neolithic, around 3000 BC and the first phase of the monument consisted of an open space surrounded by a circular ditch and an inner and outer earth bank. This formed the actual 'henge', though as mentioned in Chapter One it is not really a henge in the strict sense of the word. Fifty-six holes were dug in a circle that followed the inner bank and they probably contained wooden posts (named the 'Aubrey Holes' after John Aubrey, the 17th century antiquarian who discovered them). In the next phase of Stonehenge, which was probably built sometime after 2900 BC, a series of rather confusing post holes reveal the existence of wooden structures, though their actual form is unclear. The third phase of the monument is of great importance because it was when the huge stones at Stonehenge were erected (the 'Sarcen Circle' and the 'Trilithons'), but these were not the first stones to be raised at Stonehenge. The third phase of the monument lasted from c. 2400-1900 BC and the first stones to be erected during this period comprise of a double arc of standing stones known as the 'bluestones', which were probably re-arranged in different settings at least four times during this period.

It is known that this rock originates in the Preseli Mountains which are situated in north Pembrokeshire in south-west Wales. Many archaeologists believe that the bluestones were transported to Stonehenge by people who made an epic journey from the Preseli Mountains – bringing them hundreds of miles by land, sea and river. Some archaeologists however, feel that this idea is too incredulous (perhaps underestimating the abilities of Early Bronze Age people) and that the stones were brought to Salisbury Plain by glacial action. It is a debate that will probably never be resolved but the former theory garners more support. Also as mentioned above, those responsible for the transportation of the bluestones may have been Beaker people from Wales and this is suggested by the grave of the 'Boscombe Bowmen'.

## The Boscombe Bowmen

In May 2003, another Beaker burial was discovered on Boscombe Down in Wiltshire and again, a fine array of artefacts were found in the grave. It was also a very unusual Beaker burial. Normally, Beaker graves contain one or two skeletons but this grave, which was designed for one person held the remains of seven individuals. In the grave there were three adult males, a teenage male and three children (one of whom had been cremated). Interestingly, the male skulls all had distinctive small bones in them known as 'Wormian' bones and this almost certainly indicates that they were related.

This burial also contained a large number of fine Beakers, which had largely been decorated using cord and as mentioned above these are known as All-Over-Corded-Ware (AOC Beakers), which date to the start of the Beaker period. These Beakers are very rare in the British Isles and are more common in continental Europe and to find such large numbers of Beakers is very unusual, though there were a large number of people buried in the grave. Other rare examples of AOC Beakers were found in the grave of the Amesbury Archer, not far away (this perhaps indicates that there is some kind of link between the two burials). Also found in the grave were five barbed and tanged arrowheads, which led to the people buried here being called the 'Boscombe Bowmen'. Other finds were a boar's tusk and a bone 'toggle' that may have been used to fasten clothing or as an ornament and only one other example has been found in a Beaker burial in the British Isles (at Barnack, in Cambridgeshire). However like the AOC Beakers these toggles are fairly common in Beaker graves in continental Europe.

The evidence therefore indicated that the Boscombe Bowmen also came from the continent, but subsequent scientific analysis of the teeth produced something of a surprise – it was apparent from the analysis of the isotopes that they could only have come from two areas – Wales or the

Lake District. This discovery was highly intriguing because the Bowmen were buried at around the same time the Welsh bluestones were being erected at Stonehenge (although no radiocarbon dates for the burial are available at the time of writing it is likely to date to c. 2400 BC). While this scientific evidence does not definitely prove that the Boscombe Bowmen were involved in the transportation of the bluestones from the Preseli Mountains to Stonehenge, it does lend strong support for this theory. The idea is further strengthened by the fact that settings of bluestones similar to those found at Stonehenge are also known from the Preseli Mountains and on Skomer Island off the coast of Pembrokeshire. It therefore seems likely that the Bowmen were actually born in Wales, though whether their parents were native Welsh is hard to say. The evidence found in the grave of the bowmen indicates indeniable links with Central Europe, which suggests that their parents immigrated from the Continent and that the bowmen probably spent their childhood somewhere in Wales. Interestingly, the analysis of the Bowmen's teeth also revealed that they had lived in one place until they were about six and then moved to another area until they were in their early teens. After this they moved again to the Stonehenge region, where as we have seen they ended their days. Such evidence suggests perhaps that the Beaker people were frequently on the move and may lend further support to the idea that the Beaker period in the British Isles was initiated by newcomers from the continent.

### Beaker burials in the peninsula

The situation in Wales during the Beaker period is perhaps not as clear-cut as it is in many other parts of the British Isles during this time. For example, in many parts of the British Isles during the Beaker period, Neolithic tombs fell out of use, but in the west of Wales some of the megalithic tombs continued to be used and early Beaker pottery is found in them. It also appears that typical Beaker burials were not particularly common (though this could be down to a lack of excavation and later destruction) and they appear somewhat later than elsewhere in the British Isles. Also, they do not appear to have been as well furnished as other Beaker burials and the characteristic tanged copper daggers and

*Gyrn Ddu (45)*

*Gyrn Ddu (46)*

*Gyrn Ddu (47)*

*Gyrn Ddu (48)*

*Bwlch Mawr (49)*

*Bwlch Mawr (50)*

*Mynydd Mynytho (51)*

*Cefngraeanog (52)*

*Mynydd Rhiw (53)*

*Mynydd Rhiw (54)*

*Mynydd Rhiw (55)*

*Garn Fadrun (56)*

*Gyrn Ddu (57)*

*Gyrn Ddu (58)*

*Bronmiod (59)*

*Bronmiod (60)*

*Clynnog Fawr (61)*

*Clynnog Fawr (62)*

*Tre'r Ceiri (63-65)*

122

*Tre'r Ceiri (66-69)*

*Garn Boduan (70-73)*

*Garn Fadrun (74-78)*

*View from Craig y Ddinas (79)*

*Craig y Ddinas (80)*

*Craig y Ddinas (81)*

*Garn Pentyrch (82)*

*Garn Pentyrch (83)*

*Garn Pentyrch (84)*

bracers appear to be lacking from Beaker graves. A small number of 'riveted' copper knives (which are similar to the tanged examples but later in date) have been found in Welsh Beaker graves and a stone bracer was found in a burial cairn near Carno in Powys. However it was found in association with two Collared Urns and a Food Vessel, which were used after the end of the Beaker period. Another bracer was found at Llantrithyd in Glamorgan, although its original context is unclear. Nevertheless, several barbed and tanged arrowheads have been found in Welsh Beaker graves (of which there are around forty) and it is quite possible that other bracers or even tanged daggers will be found in undiscovered Beaker burials in Wales. We are fortunate that a handful of Beaker burials were found in our area of interest and these will now be discussed.

### The Penarth Beaker burial

In 1910, at Penarth Farm, which is situated near Aberdesach on the western coast of the peninsula in Arfon, a workman laying a new stone wall in a field discovered a cist grave. The cist, which was covered by a large capstone, was oriented north-south with its side stones measuring nearly 3ft long, while the northern and southern head stones were each about 2ft wide. The grave was about 1.5 ft in depth and a well-preserved Beaker that was almost complete was found lying in its southern end. Also found a couple of days later, was a fragment of another Beaker and it was apparent from the decoration on this piece that it came from a Beaker that was of a different type to the original. No burial mound was found covering the grave, but there may once have been one as those who worked on the farm had often found large stones close to the grave.

No other grave goods were found in the cist and the evidence for human burial in the grave was very meagre. Nevertheless, some small fragments of bone were discovered in the soil that had filled the grave and were examined by a Dr. Owen of nearby Penygroes, who felt that they belonged to either a child or a dog. It seems more probable however, that the bones belonged to a child, although dogs have been found in other Beaker burials.

## The Penarth Beakers

In 1957, W.E. Griffiths published an article that set out to reclassify and discuss the origins of Beakers in Wales. He basically followed an earlier classification of Welsh Beakers by Dr. H. N. Savory, but made further revisions (we do not really need to worry about these) of the three main classes of Welsh Beakers that Savory had labelled A, B and C Beakers. Although his scheme has undergone some later revision it still provides a useful basis for interpreting the different types of Welsh Beakers.

The first Beaker found in the cist belongs to his C class, which he describes as 'ovoid jars with splayed necks' and although these types of Beakers are rare in Wales, other examples have been found in burials, which provide poignant reminders of the fragilty of prehistoric life. In a cist discovered near Treharris in Glamorgan, a C Beaker accompanied the skull of a child, while in another C Beaker cist grave found near Ludchurch in Pembrokeshire, a man, woman, two children (one of whom was newly born) and a dog were buried and it may be that they died at the same time in tragic circumstances.

The C Beaker found in the cist at Penarth was similar in from and decoration to Beakers found in Devon and Somerset, but more closely resembled a Beaker from Norham in Northumberland. Edward Roberts, who examined the Penarth C Beaker, suggested that the decoration on it had been made with a sharpened stick or bone. The fragment of beaker which also came from the cist at Penarth, was well enough preserved to allow a reconstruction of its original form and decoration and it was found to have belonged to an A Beaker. Griffiths describes A Beakers as 'bipartite or waisted vessels with a globular and a relatively tall neck, half the height of the entire vase in the best examples'. The decoration on the A Beaker fragment consists of 'saltires' orSt Andrew's crosses as they are more commonly known and quite similar decoration can be seen on an A Beaker found at Llanbabo in Ynys Môn. A Beakers decorated with saltires are also quite common in southern England and examples have been found in Wiltshire and Somerset.

## The Llithfaen Beaker burial

In November 1947, in the village of Llithfaen (which lies below Yr Eifl in Llŷn), a gang of workmen were digging trenches for water pipes when they discovered a Beaker burial in a cist grave. The cist was again orientated north-south and it side stones measured around 3.5 ft long, with the northern and southern end stones measuring some 1.5 ft and 2.5 ft wide respectively (the cist was therefore trapezoidal in shape). The capstone of the grave was also found and this was about 8 in. thick. The grave was around 1.5ft deep and lying inside it was the badly preserved skeleton of an adult male (though his teeth were in good condition) with an intact Beaker by his feet. Dr. W. Charles Evans studied the skeleton and came to the conclusion that he was aged over 21 at the time of his death and measured some 6ft. in height. In a later note on the burial in *Archaeologia Cambrensis* (1985), Frances Lynch states he was over 25 and so he may have been aged around 30 when he died. The man had been placed in the grave lying on his right side with his head pointing north, which seems to have been a common custom in Beaker burials and was probably related to religious ideas about the sun.

## The Llithfaen Beaker

The Beaker found in the cist is of a light buff colour, measures about 7.5 ins. in height and belongs to the A Beaker class. The decoration on the Beaker is said to have been made by impressing the wet clay with a wooden or bone comb. The zones of decoration on the Llithfaen Beaker, which feature pendants or voided and filled triangles, are also seen on A and C Beakers from Yorkshire, north-east England and south-east Scotland.

H. Harold Hughes who wrote up the Llithfaen Beaker burial in the 1939 edition of *Archaeologia Cambrensis*, also records that 'Dr Evans informs me that two similar burials are said to have been found within the last fifty years not more than fifteen or twenty yards from the present find'. Two fragments from a broken 'earthenware pot' and human bones from one of the graves were said to have been kept for many years by a Mr. Evans who ran the Llithfaen Post Office.

It seems extremely likely that these finds came from one of a pair of Beaker cist graves, though what happened to both the finds and the graves is a mystery. Perhaps someone in Llithfaen (a relative of Mr. Evans?) still has the Beaker fragments and the bones. It is possible that the cist graves still survive and that further evidence for the Beaker people still lies below the ground at Llithfaen, waiting to be rediscovered.

### Beaker Immigrants in the peninsula?

It is hard to say with any real certainty whether the Beaker graves at Penarth Farm and Llithfaen mark the burial places of Beaker people who had immigrated into the peninsula from elsewhere. However, as we saw with the Amesbury Archer and the Boscombe Bowmen, scientific analysis has shown that not only did Beaker people migrate into the British Isles from the continent, but native Beaker people in the British Isles also migrated to other parts of the country. It is therefore worth examining the Penarth and Llithfaen Beaker burials as they may help to provide some clues as to the origin of the people in these graves.

In regard to the Beaker burial at Penarth Farm, we only have the intact Beaker and Beaker fragment from which to draw conclusions and as we saw above, the intact Penarth Beaker was of the C class. Griffiths suggests in his article that the earliest C Beakers in the British Isles are found in Scotland and that they were brought by immigrants from Holland and the Rhineland. He is somewhat vague on how they reached Wales, but says that they are 'late survivals of a type, whose main development took place earlier and in areas far to the north of Wales'

With the Llithfaen Beaker burial recorded by H. Harold Hughes we are perhaps on firmer ground as to the identity of the individual buried in the grave, though as to the other Beaker burials found nearby nothing can really be said, as the evidence appears to be lacking. As we have seen, an A Beaker was found in the cist at Llithfaen and it shows similar decoration to A Beakers from Yorkshire, Northumberland and south-east Scotland.

Griffiths rightly notes that there are two main

concentrations of A Beakers in Wales, with the first in East Glamorgan and the Black Mountains (Brecknock) and the second in Gwynedd. These two distinct concentrations do seem to indicate Beaker settlers arriving in Wales and Griffiths suggests that the A Beakers in northern Wales 'could be explained as the result of a westward spread from East Anglia, Yorkshire or Northumberland, where zigzags, fingernail impressions and other features of the Welsh pottery are all represented'. However, we should also remember that the fragment of the A Beaker found at Penarth Farm displays saltires that are not uncommon on A Beakers in southern England and that its decoration quite closely resembles that found on an A Beaker in Ynys Môn. Whether this evidence indicates immigration into northern Wales by Beaker groups from southern England can never be known, but it is a possibility that should be considered.

In regard to the ultimate origin of the Welsh A Beakers Griffiths feels that there is no real evidence to suggest that they were introduced from the continent and therefore concludes that they were a native development that began in one of the above areas. However, whether Griffiths is correct in his assumption is hard to say.

Although Griffiths' suggestion that the northern Welsh A Beakers arrived from northern and eastern parts of England is perfectly feasible it does not prove that the man buried in the cist at Llithfaen came from this area. There may be a way though, that this could be achieved. It is to be hoped that the skeletal evidence from the Llithfaen Beaker burial still survives, as it would be possible to analyse the teeth in the same way that those of the Amesbury Archer and the Boscombe Bowmen. This analysis could therefore hopefully provide us with a good idea of the birthplace of the man buried in the Llithfaen Beaker grave.

As Frances Lynch has pointed out, the Beakers found in Beaker burials in Wales are mainly considered to be types that belong to the later Beaker period. This perhaps suggests that Griffiths' settlers from southern, northern and eastern England did bring the Beaker culture into Wales some time after it had first become established in these areas. Nevertheless, there are some early Beaker burials in Wales, though whether they mark the graves of continental immigrants is unknown. In this respect, perhaps we should not forget the Boscombe Bowmen. As we have seen, the archaeological evidence indicates that they may have been related to continental Beaker immigrants who arrived in Wales during the early Beaker period. As is often the way when examining significant changes in prehistoric society, it is hard to unravel the truth from the tangled threads of archaeological evidence.

## Other Evidence for the Beaker people in the peninsula

Although not plentiful, we do have some other evidence that can be connected with the Beaker people in the peninsula and some of the finds are quite impressive. The first of these to be mentioned is the barbed and tanged arrowhead found in 1922 by W.J. Hemp on a sheep track on the slopes of Yr Eifl. As we have seen, these arrowheads were used by the Beaker people and placed in their graves. It is perhaps interesting to note that the Beaker grave at Llithfaen only lies about a mile from the where the arrowhead was discovered The discovery of the Stonehenge Archer has shown that these distinctive arrowheads were used to kill people (though they must also have been used for hunting) and hint at an aggressive and male-dominated Beaker society. The stone 'battle-axes', which also make their first appearance during the Beaker period, perhaps provide us with firmer evidence of a war-like society. Although battle-axes may have been more emblematic of male status, it seems likely that they were sometimes used in violent encounters during the Beaker period. These weapons are fearsome looking and would certainly have inflicted fatal injuries when used in anger. Stone battle-axes have not been found with any Beaker burials from Wales, though a number have been discovered as stray finds and a fine example was found near Chwilog in Eifionydd. A curious miniature battle-axe was also discovered at Pant-glas, which lies very close to the western boundary of the Snowdonia National Park.

Also associated with the Beaker people are the fascinating 'lunulae' which are thought to date to the later, or 'Classical' phase of the Beaker period (c. 2200-2000 BC). These sheet gold ornaments which are assumed to have been collars of some kind have a similar shape to that of the crescent moon – hence the name – and seem to be confined to countries along the Atlantic Seaways (in particular Ireland). We are particularly fortunate to have an example of lunula from our study area, as this is the only known example that has so far been found in Wales.

The lunula was found in the late nineteenth century in the edge of a peat bog on Tir y Dewin farm (still marked on the modern OS map), which is located near Bryncir on the eastern edge of the peninsula. In her detailed study of the lunulae, Dr Joan Taylor (who is the leading authority on Bronze Age goldwork in the British Isles) classified them into three distinct groupings: 'Classical', 'Unaccomplished' and 'Provincial'. Dr Taylor says of the first type, that they 'are so named for their excellence of craftsmanship' and that they may have been made in regional workshops, where master craftsmen were assisted by groups of apprentices. In contrast, as their name suggests, the Unaccomplished lunulae are of poorer quality in terms of both shape and decoration, though it seems that both types were made in Ireland. The final Provincial group, however, were made in western regions of Britain and the example found at Tir y Dewin is of this type. Taylor tells us that the Provincial group 'generally has the greatest gold content and is well beaten, of stiffer sheet and decorated with a simpler range of Beaker motifs'.

It may also be interesting to note that in Welsh, Tir y Dewin means 'The Wizard's Land', and it could be speculated that this name may suggest that a druid once lived in this area in the time of the ancient Celts. However, it would probably be pushing the borders of credulity too far to suggest that the wizard in question may have been a priest or shaman of the Beaker people who once wore the lunula found here.

Lunulae are not found in Beaker burials and although their actual function is unclear, Taylor has suggested that they may have been symbolic of the status of a ruling family or powerful Beaker priests. Alternatively, she has suggested that they may have been worn on statues of deities that functioned as cult objects. Whatever the reality behind the lunulae of the British Isles, Taylor's study of them has revealed little signs of wear and as she points out, this indicates that they were only used on special occasions. This perhaps strengthens the case for their use as ornaments placed on cult objects.

The standing stones of Llŷn, Arfon and Eifionydd should also not be forgotten when considering other evidence for the Beaker people in the peninsula. We have already seen the distinct possibility that Beaker people from Wales erected the standing stones known as the bluestones at Stonehenge. Archaeological evidence also suggests that Beaker people may have erected the stone circles inside the awesome Neolithic henge monument at Avebury in Wiltshire. In 1930, Ben and Maud Cunnington started their major excavations at Avebury and near a pit that had held a huge, fallen megalith, they discovered a Beaker burial. Further Beaker burials were found near the two parallel rows of standing stones known as the 'Kennet Avenue' (now partially reconstructed), which ran from the southern entrance of the henge to the two stone circles at the 'Sanctuary', some 1.5 miles away on Overton Hill. At the foot of two of the avenue's standing stones, two Beaker burials in cist graves were found, while at the Sanctuary, a young girl was buried with a Beaker at the foot of one of the stones in the inner circle. It is quite possible that she was ritually sacrificed and buried in the Sanctuary as a 'dedicatory' offering to the deities worshipped by the Beaker people.

Further archaeological evidence points to the involvement of the Beaker people at major Neolithic religious sites. For example at the Mount Pleasant Henge a massive timber palisade and a probable stone circle was erected during the Beaker period, while at West Kennet long barrow, a huge façade of megalithic stones was erected and the tomb was blocked up.

The above evidence indicates that there is a connection between the arrival of the Beaker people in the British Isles and what Michael Parker Pearson has called 'a phase of monumentalization in stone'. It may well be that the Beaker people were usurping the old, Neolithic ritual and ceremonial sites and building their own spectacular monuments, so that they could achieve a position of power and authority among the Late Neolithic communities of the British Isles.

It is perhaps unlikely that it was Beaker people who actually raised standing stones in the peninsula and more probable that they reveal a response to new religious ideas by the small, indigenous communities who lived here during the Early Bronze Age. Nevertheless the former idea cannot be completely discarded and perhaps one day, archaeological excavation may bring us closer to answering this question.

Finally, it should also be noted that some of the Early Bronze Age burial cairns found in the peninsula (which will be discussed in the next chapter), may well have their origins in the Beaker period. As Frances Lynch has noted, a number of burial mounds in Wales 'show a sequence of re-use going back to a 'founding father' accompanied by a Beaker, the distinctive symbol of these 'new men' – whether they were truly strangers or perhaps local leaders adopting new strategies'. As far as I am aware, the burial cairns of the peninsula have not yielded any evidence of the Beaker people, but underneath the mounds of stone that sit on its beautiful hills and peaks there may still be members of this ancient and innovative society waiting to be discovered.

Chapter 7

# Cairns for the Dead

Although many Bronze Age burial cairns in Wales have been destroyed because they provide excellent building material for field walls, many still survive and they are an ubiquitous feature of the uplands. Fortunately, the landscape of the peninsula does not prove an exception to the rule and several burial cairns can be found on its hills and peaks. As in other parts of Wales, the burial cairns of Llŷn, Arfon and Eifionydd survive in varying degrees of preservation and in general have suffered at the hands of farmers and 'treasure hunters'. However, whether the cairns are well preserved or badly damaged by later activity, they stand as a testament to an ancient people and provide us with insights into their society.

It is apparent that as in Yorkshire during the Late Neolithic, large barrows containing individual burials were also a feature of this period in Wales and beneath a barrow at Four Crosses near Welshpool, three individuals were buried in a huge pit. It had been assumed that the barrow dated to the Early Bronze Age, but subsequent radiocarbon dating indicates that the deceased were placed in the pit as separate acts of interment between 3200-3100 BC. Another Late Neolithic barrow, which also covered an individual burial, was discovered not far away at Trelystan. However, as in England, such burials were rare and it was not until the Beaker period in Wales that the practice of individual burial under burial mounds became 'common' (as we have previously seen only around forty Beaker burials are known from Wales – though this may not be a true reflection of reality).

Whatever the truth regarding the number of Beaker burials in Wales, by the onset of the second millennium BC, the common burial rite in Wales was interment under a mound of earth (barrow) or stones (cairn) – as it was elsewhere in the British Isles. By this time in Wales, cremation had also replaced the burial rite of inhumation, but why this was, is unclear. It may be perhaps, that in time the influence of the Beaker people waned as their descendants became assimilated into the indigenous population of Early Bronze Age Wales. Thus, although the Beaker practice of burial under a mound was preferred, there was also a return to the native practice of cremating the dead, which had been the dominant funerary rite in the western, Neolithic tombs.

It was mentioned at the end of Chapter Six that some burial mounds in Wales originated in the Beaker period but were then subsequently re-used as later burials were inserted into them. We have clear examples of this sequential process in action, with the burial mounds excavated at Merddyn Gwyn in Anglesey and Sutton in Glamorgan.

At Merddyn Gwyn on Anglesey, the initial phase of the monument was marked by an individual Beaker burial. Subsequently, this cairn was enlarged and a cremation in a 'Food Vessel' (distinctive pots used in the Early Bronze Age) was placed in the burial mound. Finally, two cremations in Collared Urns were inserted into the top of the enlarged mound.

The burial mound at Sutton followed a similar development to its counterpart at Merddyn Gwyn. The first burial in the monument consisted of a child accompanied by a late Beaker and seven barbed and tanged arrowheads, placed under a small cairn. Next, the burial of a man took the place of the child and the cairn was enlarged. In the final stages of the monument, it was further enlarged by the addition of an earth mound. This was surrounded by a stone wall and a 'Pygmy Cup' (small pots which may have been used in funerary rituals as containers for burning unknown substances) and Collared Urns were inserted into the original cairn.

However, by the early centuries of the second millennium BC, these 'Beaker-inspired' burial mounds were no longer seen, and now, the common practice was to insert a number of burials into a barrow or cairn that lacked a primary, central burial. Such burial mounds are more commonly found in north-west Britain and Ireland and some were used for hundreds of years, with burials still being made in barrows and cairns in the Late Bronze Age, c. 1100 BC. Unfortunately, interpreting the different burials placed in barrows and cairns is far from easy and as Frances Lynch has said: '[i]deally it should be possible to deduce that they were buried as a group, rather than individually, but the evidence is seldom that satisfactory'.

The standard type of cairn built in Wales during the Early Bronze Age consisted of a simple circular heap of stone which could vary greatly in size. Large boulders often ringed the cairns, though these are now difficult to find because the loose boulders used to build the main body of the cairns have often collapsed on top of them. The other types of cairn that can be found in Wales are platform, kerb, and walled cairns. The former monuments, which are shaped like low drums are unfortunately, often hard to recognise because of later damage. Kerb cairns, which are very small in comparison to the other types of cairn, are also later in date and seem to have been built in the latter half of the second millennium around 1300 BC. Walled cairns such as the one mentioned above at Sutton are not common and were a regional tradition confined to southern Wales.

It is also possible to identify architectural features underneath both barrows and cairns and complicated arrangements of wooden and stone settings can often be found. The exact nature of these arrangements is not completely clear but some must relate to ritual and ceremonial activity that took place before they were built. A probable example of such activity has been found during the excavation of a cairn at Cefn Caer Euni (Meirionnydd), where a thick layer of clay covering a pile of settlement debris was found underneath the cairn.

Although this chapter is primarily concerned with the burial cairns of the peninsula it should not be forgotten that barrows were also raised in its landscape during the Early Bronze Age. Unfortunately, as is the case elsewhere in Wales, the barrows of the peninsula have not stood the test of time quite as well as their stone counterparts and are scarce. Nevertheless there is a probable Early Bronze Age barrow on Ynys Enlli and a large, earthen mound that can still be seen

near Trwyn y Ffosle on Mynydd Cilan in Llŷn may also be a
barrow that covers a burial (or burials) from this time.
Mention should also be made of the barrow cemetery near
Efailnewydd in Llŷn, which appears to have contained three,
typical barrows of the Early Bronze Age. Although the
barrows have now been virtually ploughed out, limited
investigations at the site have revealed that they were
around 25-30m in diameter and were surrounded by ring-
ditches. Environmental analysis showed that the barrows
were constructed of turf and suggested that originally, they
stood in an environment of open grassland. Interestingly, the
Royal commission tells us that 'an unconfirmed antiquarian
notice of funerary urns, thought be Roman, is thought to
relate to these monuments'. If the urns were indeed Roman,
they reveal that people still regarded the barrow cemetery as
a sacred place some two thousand years after people of the
Early Bronze Age buried their dead here. Whether the
original burials have survived is not known, though it is
perhaps unlikely. Nevertheless, it would certainly be worth
investigating this site in more detail, to see what secrets may
lie waiting to be discovered below the ground. Finally, it also
seems probable that a number of the circular cropmarks that
can be seen on aerial photographs of the peninsula represent
former barrows that have been destroyed by later
agricultural activity.


## THE BURIAL CAIRNS OF LLŶN,
## ARFON AND EIFIONYYD

### Mynydd Carnguwch (41)

I would hazard a guess that this is one of finest burial cairns
to be found in the whole of Wales. This hugely impressive
cairn is located on the summit of Mynydd Carnguwch,
which is a distinct, dome-shaped hill that lies just below yr
Eifl near the road that leads into Llŷn. The cairn measures
about 20 ft. in height and from north-east to south-west is
around 130 ft. in diameter, while from west to east it
measures about 100 ft. Allowing for the fact that the cairn
has collapsed somewhat over time and has probably

supplied local farmers with building material, it must have been even more imposing than it is today. The cairn was built around a natural outcrop of rock that rises from the summit of Mynydd Carnguwch and there are fantastic views from the cairn down the length of Llŷn, along the coast of Arfon towards Ynys Môn and into the heart of Snowdonia.

A revetment wall surrounds the central part of the cairn but it is not clear whether this would have been visible or whether it was an inner architectural feature that was hidden inside the cairn. W.J. Hemp suggested that this revetment could possibly represent the lower half of a 'solid truncated conical tower 10 or 15 ft. high' and drew a parallel with Late Bronze Age burial mounds in Brittany, which were shaped like this. However, although it is possible that the cairn was tower-like, it seems more probable that the cairn was of the standard type found in Wales.

The cairn has a large hole at its centre that no doubt represents the attempts of later treasure hunters to reach the burials placed in the cairn. Whether they were successful in their attempts cannot be said, but it seems highly likely that this cairn has not yet yielded up its secrets. The sheer size of this cairn almost certainly means that it will never be excavated scientifically, but this is not a bad thing because it is a superb and distinctive monument, that plays an important part in the ancient history of the peninsula.

It may also be worth mentioning an interesting ritual that once took place near the cairn in more recent times. Elfed Gruffydd tells us in his fascinating *Llŷn*, that it was formerly the custom to light a huge bonfire on top of Mynydd Carnguwch on Halloween and that once the bonfire had been lit, 'all those present would rush headlong for home before a fearsome cow known as Hwch Ddu Gwta *(the Black Sow with the short tail?)* caught them'. It is well known that today's Halloween represents the survival into modern times of the ancient festival of Samhain, during which time fires were lit to drive away evil spirits. Is it possible that the Halloween bonfire on Mynydd Carnguwch preserves traces of rituals and beliefs that are far more ancient?

### Tre'r Ceiri *(42)*

This badly ruined cairn is located at the highest point within the walls of the magnificent Iron Age fort of Tre'r Ceiri. It has again been suggested that this cairn represents the remains of a tower and that it may have been built at the same time as the fort. This theory was probably inspired by what appeared to be sections of straight facing in the cairn, but excavation of the cairn in 1956, showed it to be incorrect. In any case, a tower built within the fort would be an unnecessary extravagance in a location that already provided superb all-round views over miles of countryside. As mentioned above, the cairn is in poor condition and sadly, it is now little more than a haphazard spread of large stones. However, is still possible to tell that some care went into the building of the cairn, and that it is built of naturally curved slabs of stone. As to the original size of the cairn it is hard to say, but it is likely that it was fairly substantial.

### Yr Eifl *(43, 44, 45)*

Of the two cairns that survive on the western summit of Yr Eifl, one is in very poor condition and resembles the Tre'r Ceiri cairn. However, the other, which is situated close to the ruined one, is in better condition. Although a modern Ordnance Survey pillar has been built on top of the cairn, it is still quite an impressive monument being some 70 ft. in diameter and about 15 ft. in height. As is often the case the cairn appears to have been dug into at some time in the past, as evidenced by the large hole in its centre. These cairns are not easy to reach, but the views from them can only be described as superlative. To the north-east you can see the coast of Arfon curving round towards Ynys Môn, to the east, the mountains and hills of Snowdonia and mid Wales march away towards Pembrokeshire, while to the south-west, Llŷn unfolds before you as it stretches towards the peninsula's end at Ynys Enlli.

### Gyrn Ddu *(45, 46, 47, 48)*

Three cairns can be seen on Gyrn Ddu, with one on its western summit and the other two located about half a mile away on its eastern summit. The south-western cairn is located on the striking rock formation that marks the western summit and is very small in comparison to the two cairns found on the eastern summit, and also the other cairns found elsewhere in the peninsula.

Therefore, at first sight, the cairn appears to be a modern one such as those built by hill walkers. Nevertheless, although some of the stones making up the cairn are likely to have been placed there by modern hillwalkers, some are large and would require a lot of effort to lift. Also the cairn is marked as an archaeological monument on the Ordnance Survey map of the peninsula and so it seems likely that it was once bigger, but is now reduced in size because stones have collapsed from its main body. Nevertheless, although not an impressive monument today, the cairn still provides us with a reminder of the religious practices that took place on the summit of Gyrn Ddu some 4000 years ago.

The 2 cairns on the eastern summit of Gryn Ddu survive in contrasting states of preservation, with one being badly damaged by later activity and the other surviving in a damaged, but fair condition. Although the badly damaged cairn now consists of a low mound of large stones, it would once have been a substantial monument like its nearby companion, which still stands at around 8 ft. high and measures some 45 ft. in diameter. A modern field wall crosses both cairns and it is obvious that many of the stones in this wall came from the two cairns and the better-preserved cairn has noticeable depressions in it, which lie either side of the wall where it crosses the body of the cairn. As with all the other burial cairns in the peninsula, these two monuments are located in a position that offers breathtaking views of the peninsula and beyond.

### Bwlch Mawr *(49, 50)*

This cairn is situated on the summit of Bwlch Mawr, which rises above the village of Clynnog Fawr in Arfon. Like Gyrn Ddu, the summit of Bwlch Mawr features striking formations of granite and the possible significance of this will be discussed when we come to look at the location of the cairns. Although damaged, this monument provides us with a rare example of the constructional techniques employed by the cairn builders and the cairn at Tre'r Ceiri is likely to have been built in the same way.

It appears that a central cairn – which probably still covers a burial/s – was raised first and then this central component was ringed with flatter, curving stones, which were built up around it. One large and narrow stone lying at 90° degrees to these stones appears to have been built into the inner ring of stones and another similar stone can be seen lying loose on top of the ring. It is possible that these were deliberate constructional devices, though they could be fortuitous inclusions in the body of the outer cairn. This cairn offers particularly good views of the countryside of Eifionydd bordering the western edge of Snowdonia and also the coast of Arfon as it snakes away towards Caernarfon and Ynys Môn. The peaks of Gyrn Goch and Gyrn Ddu can also be seen rising dramatically to the south-west, while beyond, Mynydd Carnguwch with its crowning cairn rises from the low-lying farmland at the north-eastern end of Llŷn.

## Foel Gron (51)

his fairly modest cairn is situated on the distinctive, rounded hill known as Foel Gron (which marks the remains of an ancient volcano) that rises above the village of Mynytho on the eastern coast of Llŷn. It is hard to say for sure though, whether this monument is actually a burial cairn of the Early Bronze Age as it is not marked on the OS map and there is no reference to it in the literature. Neverthless, the cairn is in a location that mirrors that of the other burial cairns of the peninsula - i.e. it is located on a distinctive peak that gives superb, wide-ranging views. Also, a number of the stones that make up the cairn are very large and would definitely have required more than one person to move them, so it seems unlikely that the cairn was built by hillwalkers. It is possible therfore, that this monument was built in the Early Bronze Age and covers a burial. However, one problem remains - if this monument is a burial cairn, why does it not appear to have been plundered by treasure hunters? It is not a particularly large monument and it is also easy to reach, so it is hard to see why it should have escaped the attentions of such people. For the moment then, the truth behind this cairn will have to remain hidden - unless anybody knows different?

**Cefngraeanog** *(52)*
It is likely that this cairn represents one of the smaller kerbed cairns, which as mentioned above, are later in date than the other types of cairns found in Wales. Today, the cairn has suffered damage due to agricultural activity (a modern field wall crosses the edge of the cairn), but it is still possible to see a number of the kerb stones that surround the cairn, which is now about 2 ft. high. Humps and bumps nearby mark the remains of another cairn and as mentioned in Chapter 5, a fine standing stone is also located close by – though the exact relationship between the two is unclear.

The location of this cairn appears to be unusual when compared to the other examples mentioned in this chapter. Unlike them, it is situated in farmland (on the eastern edge of the peninsula, near the pass which leads to Clynnog Fawr) and not on a significant hill or mountain summit (though it is situated on a low ridge). This fact should perhaps alert us to the possibility that there may have been many other cairns (and barrows) in the peninsula, which were situated in more low-lying situations nearer settlements.

**Mynydd Rhiw** *(53, 54, 55)*
The remains of four cairns can still be seen not far from the summit of Mynydd Rhiw and mark an Early Bronze Age cairn cemetery, commonly found in the uplands of Wales. Three of the cairns are badly ruined and now basically little more than spreads of stone, but one is still fairly well preserved and stands around 3.5m high. The cairns are situated on a ridge that runs across the headland from the south-east to north-west and the significance of their location on this ridge will be discussed below. From the cairns there are magnificent views over the patchwork of fields that lie above Porth Neigwl and behind this, the distinctive shape of Garn Fadrun can be seen rising from the middle of Llŷn.

## Garn Fadrun (56)

Although this burial cairn is now collapsed, it is evident from the spread of stones that it would originally have been a fairly impressive monument. It is located on an outcrop of rock that rises above the concentration of huts that cluster around the middle of the inner rampart, on the western side of the summit. Like the more ruined burial cairn at Tre'r Ceiri, the example found at Garn Fadrun is also likely to date to the Early Bronze Age and was probably revered as an ancient site of the ancestors, by the Iron Age people who lived in the hillfort.

## The Significance of Location

The question we have to ask ourselves regarding the burial cairns of the peninsula, is why so many of them are located on the summits of its hills and mountains? Like all the prehistoric monuments found in this region, they were not placed in the landscape without any thought and there must be reasons why they are located in these high places. In the following section we will look at the most likely explanations that may account for the location of the burial cairns, though it should also be remembered that these are probably not exclusive of one another and that the burial cairns functioned on several levels at the same time.

## Religious Concerns

We have talked in previous chapters how hills and mountains were felt to be sacred places by many ancient and 'primitive' peoples and how it seems likely that the prehistoric people of the peninsula held similar views. Today, we look at hills and mountains from a detached, 'western' perspective, knowing that natural, geological processes have formed them. However, the Early Bronze Age people of the peninsula did not have the benefit of our knowledge and for them, high points in the landscape are likely to have been inhabited by spirits of the other-world and were probably magical, mysterious and perhaps even frightening places. There are two burial cairn locations that stand out in this respect – the summit of Bwlch Mawr and the western summit of Gyrn Ddu. Even today, from a modern viewpoint, the rock formations found on the summits of these mountains have a fantastic, otherworldly quality about them and must have had an even greater effect on the Early Bronze Age people of the peninsula. In the Early Bronze Age (and probably in previous prehistoric periods) these summits may well have been mythological places that were linked with ancestral or other spirit powers.

### Symbols of Power?

Although as mentioned previously, the barrows and cairns of Wales contain multiple burials, as with the megalithic tombs of the Neolithic not everyone can have been afforded the privilege of being buried in one. Even allowing for the fact that the Early Bronze population of Wales was significantly smaller than today's and many burial mounds have been destroyed, there would still surely be more surviving in the landscape – particularly in the uplands – if this funerary rite was not socially exclusive.

Peter Crew has said in his report on the excavation of a group of mountain top cairns on Drosgl near Llanllechid in Gwynedd, 'mountain top burial seems to be exclusively a phenomenon of the Bronze Age, perhaps reserved for individuals of especial importance'. It seem highly likely that these individuals were important because they occupied positions at the top of a ranked society and that such a society existed in the peninsula during the Early Bronze Age.

Following on from this suggestion, Christopher Tilley feels that on Bodmin Moor, the burial cairns found on and near the distinctive Tors mark the existence of 'a small, but significant, social élite' who were quite deliberately building cairns in the landscape, as a means of articulating and reinforcing their authority. Tilley further says in regard to this theory: '[a]ppropriating the Tors and controlling access to their embedded spirit powers and ancestral associations became part and parcel of the exercise of power and social control'.

Of course, it could be argued, that the burial cairns mark the funerary monuments of people who had won great renown in life for reasons that are now lost to us. However, the long history of the worldwide use of religious monuments as symbols of power suggests that the views of scholars such as Tilley hit closer to the mark. Ethnographic studies also perhaps provide some support for such views. For example the Mapuche people of south-central Chile built burial mounds in which chiefs, shamans and wealthy men were buried. These occur as isolated monuments and in clusters and in one such cluster overlooking the Lumaco Valley, there are 14 burial mounds, which are thought to contain the burials of a local dynasty of dead chiefs who ruled for some 400 years. Further evidence gathered from the Mapuche also reminds us that rituals and ceremonies are likely to have taken place at the cairns of the peninsula. During the building of the burial mounds shamans and relatives of the dead chief danced around his burial place and performed animal sacrifices and bloodletting on it. Finally layers of soil were placed on top, which was symbolic of the of the spirit's journey to the upper world, where the ancestors lived. As with the burial cairns of the peninsula, most of the barrows of the Mapuche were located at high points in the landscape.

Further support for the view that the cairns of the peninsula mark the burial places of an Early Bronze Age élite is provided by the fact that even today, many of them are still substantial monuments and when complete would have been even more so. This means that much time and effort must have gone into their building, often in locations not easily reached. Although it is hard to estimate how may man-hours it took to build a large cairn, as we do not know how large the work gangs were, it is likely that it took several days at least.

Of all the burial cairns in the peninsula the one that particularly stands out as being symbolic of power, is the one found crowning the summit of Mynydd Carnguwch. The first time that I visited this monument, I was immediately struck by its huge presence and my first thought was that whoever was buried here must have been of great importance. Its great size and the fact that many huge stones have been used in its construction, indicate that this monument may have taken several weeks to build – even with a large workforce. Even today, this cairn still retains a palpable aura of power that must have been felt even more keenly by the people of the Early Bronze Age. There is perhaps no other monument in the peninsula, that brings us so close to the powerful leaders who must have lived and ruled here during the Bronze Age.

**Territorial Markers?**
Just as the megalithic tombs of the peninsula may have been used by Neolithic people as territorial markers, so too may some of the cairns have been used by its Early Bronze Age communities. As Frances Lunch has pointed out, excavation of some of the presumed burial cairns of Wales has not always revealed burial, which suggests that some were used as territorial markers – or perhaps some type of political memorial. However, we should remember that those cairns that were used as burial places may also still have functioned as territorial markers. There are some cairns in the peninsula that can not really be included in the list of possible territorial markers and the most notable example is the one found on Bwlch Mawr. Because of the nature of the summit of Bwlch Mawr, this cairn cannot be seen from the surrounding countryside and it is therefore hard to see how it could have functioned as a territorial marker. Other cairns that can be mentioned in this respect are those found on the western summit of Gyrn Ddu and on the summit of Yr Eifl. Although they can be seen from lower-lying land, at a distance, they tend to blend into the summits on which they sit.

With such cairns we are again drawn back to the idea that they were located in places in the landscape that were considered to be 'special' by the people of the Early Bronze Age. Of course, although such cairns were not so easily seen in the landscape, they could still have been used as a means of reinforcing authority and reminding people of the social order of the day. The Early Bronze Age people of the peninsula may not have been able to see some of the burial cairns under which they lived their lives, but they would be only too aware of their presence and of the powerful ancestral spirits probably associated with these monuments.

## The use of landscape

Whatever view is favoured regarding the social role of the peninsula's burial cairns, it is apparent that in some cases, their builders appear to have cleverly used the landscape in order to maximise their visibility – indicating that these monuments were intended to send out 'messages' to the people.

Perhaps the most obvious example of this can be found at the cairn cemetery on Mynydd Rhiw. The remains of the four cairns found here, which run in a line across a ridge, provide us a with a good example of how Bronze Age burial mounds were often laid out on 'false crests'. This was a classic device that was often used by the builders of burial mounds and was a deliberate act on their part. Instead of being located on the actual summit of the headland, the people who built the cairns on Mynydd Rhiw chose to locate them on this ridge, which lies some way down from the summit (there was once another cairn here, but it was destroyed by the building of the radio mast that can be seen today). It cannot be said that this is indisputably true, but it seems highly likely that the cairn builders realised that if they located the cairns on the summit of the headland, travellers crossing it from east to west (or vice versa) would not be able to see them. Today, as you follow the path to the summit, which leads from the National Trust carpark on the eastern slopes of Mynydd Rhiw, the largest cairn is easily visible on the ridge in the distance. In its original state, it would have been even more visible, as no doubt would the other cairns located on the ridge.

Similar, linear cairn cemeteries are known in many other parts of Wales and the example found on the summit of Moel Trigarn in Pembrokeshire provides a fine example. Earthen barrows were also often arranged in linear cemeteries and these are particularly notable in the Stonehenge environs. A famous example is that found at the Winterbourne Stoke crossroads, where the barrows are laid out along the axis of an earlier Neolithic long barrow. It is possible that burial mounds were arranged linearly because lines of descent were being stressed by elite families of the Early Bronze Age, who used burial mounds to reinforce and express their authority.

Another likely example of how the cairn builders of the peninsula utilised the landscape in order to 'show off' the cairns is provided by the examples found on the eastern summit of Gyrn Ddu. The eastern summit of Gyrn Ddu covers a fairly large, plateau-like area and there are a number of places that the cairns found here could have been located. However, the people responsible for the construction of the cairns found here, chose to build them on a rounded spur of land that juts out from the main area of the summit. Again, this is likely to have been a deliberate choice on their part, as this spur provides the best part on the eastern summit of Gryn Ddu, on which to show the cairns as silhouettes against the skyline. Placing the cairns elsewhere on the eastern summit would have meant that the cairns would not be visible from a distance because the nature of its topography and the western summit behind would mean that they could not always be seen in silhouette. Of course, one of the cairns cannot now be seen, but originally both cairns would have been visible from lower-lying areas of the peninsula.

The splendid monument on Mynydd Carnguwch provides another probable example of how the landscape may have been used to enhance the visibility of the burial cairns. The rounded profile of Mynydd Carnguwch and its location at the north-eastern end of Llŷn, mean that the cairn on its summit can be seen as a distinctive silhouette against the skyline from many locations in the peninsula. In comparison, the other cairns that are visible on summits have a somewhat limited range in terms of where they can be seen from.

Of course, we have to take into account the fact that the cairn on Mynydd Carnguwch is much larger than the others found in the peninsula and this therefore contributes to its greater visibility. However, as discussed above, this monument is suggestive of significant authority and although Mynydd Carnguwch is not a particularly high peak (359m), it seems likely that this location was chosen because it was the best place to display this authority. It could be argued that the builders of this monument did not realise the significance of its location, but this seems unlikely and it is hard to disagree with Stefan Bergh's statement that '[a] clearly visible monument brings ...an ever present message to all passerby's. The greater the visibility – the stronger the message. Relations of social power can thence be expressed and upheld by the erection of... spectacular monuments in dominant locations'.

Conversely however, it should also be borne in mind that some of the peninsula's burial cairns may have been located in conspicuous locations because of their wide-ranging views, rather than the fact that they could be seen from many lower-lying areas of land. As Peter Crew mentions in respect of such burial cairns in Wales, '[I]t has recently been proposed that the prominent positions for these burials may have been chosen for the sake of the view *from* the spot'. Crew tells us of the native American Chieftain, O-ma-haw who 'wished to be buried on a prominent knoll, with spectacular views overlooking the Missouri, so that he could watch over the traffic passing up and down the river'. Whether the Early Bronze Age chieftains of the peninsula had similar concerns when it came to choosing the site of their final resting place can unfortunately never be known. However, it is quite possible that in death, these leaders desired to look out over areas that were in some way special to them.

### Indicators of settlement?

As mentioned in Chapter 4, during the Early Bronze Age in Wales, people began to exploit the uplands for agricultural purposes and it was mentioned that some of the prehistoric settlements found in the peninsula's uplands probably represent the remains of farming settlements dating to this period. Further support for this idea is provided by the fact that several of the burial cairns of the peninsula are also located close to the remains of prehistoric settlements. In particular, the uplands above the coast of Arfon (i.e. Bwlch Mawr, Gyrn Goch, Gyrn Ddu and Moel Bronmiod) stand out in this respect and there is a concentration of both cairns and prehistoric settlements in this area. Admittedly, this does not prove an Early Bronze Age date for these settlements but it does suggest that some at least do date to this period and that some of the cairns may have been built by the people who lived in them. It is hard to say whether these settlements were occupied year-round, but if so, they must have been harsh places to live in during the winter months and it is perhaps more likely that they were used during the summer months, when livestock were grazed in the uplands.

## Chapter 8

# Introduction to the Iron Age

Iron appears to have been discovered in the middle of the second millennium BC, by the ancient Hittites who lived in the area now occupied by Turkey and Syria. However, they do not appear to have shared their knowledge of iron working with the outside world and it was not until the collapse of their empire around 1200 BC, that this knowledge began to gradually spread across Europe, arriving in the British Isles around 750 BC.

When one considers the huge part that iron played in driving the industrial revolution, which shaped the modern world, the significance of the Iron Age in the British Isles (c. 750 BC - AD 43) cannot be underestimated. However, for us, the real significance of the Iron Age lies in the fact that it saw the emergence of the famous Celts, who have been called the 'first fathers of Europe'. Today, the descendants of this ancient people who were spread far and wide across Europe, still live in areas along Europe's western edge and Wales, Scotland, Ireland, Brittany, Cornwall and the Isle of Man share a common Celtic heritage. This heritage reveals itself not only in art, literature and music but also and most importantly, in the speaking of Celtic languages, which are directly related to those spoken by their prehistoric ancestors.

Unfortunately, although there have been attempts to revive the ancient languages of Cornish and Manx, a general lack of interest has meant that effectively, these are 'dead' Celtic languages. Nevertheless, although English is the dominant language in Ireland and Scotland, the Celtic language of Gaelic is still alive in some areas. Likewise in Brittany, the Breton language still holds out against the French and Brittany still retains a strong and separate identity, from her larger and more powerful neighbour. However, it is the Welsh who have been most successful in retaining their language and as Alastair Moffat has pointed out, this is because 'they have long understood that without their language, their nation will fade from the map of history'. Being a native of Liverpool and spending a large amount of time in north-western Wales, I often hear the Welsh language being spoken, though my Welsh is at best, rudimentary. However, as Moffat has also said, 'if we listen hard to what the Welsh say, we can hear an echo of Britain talking 2,000 years ago' and this is something of which I am constantly aware.

The Celts originated in Central Europe, around the start of the first millennium BC, probably in the area that is today occupied by Switzerland and south-west Germany. It was here that a people with a new and distinctive material culture emerged and it is probable that they were descended from the Late Bronze Age, central European Tumulus and Urnfield cultures. These people were known as the Hallstatt culture and were first identified in a superbly rich cemetery found near the salt-mining town of Hallsatt (hence the name) in upper Austria. They were marked out by their distinctive, geometric based art and their 'princely' chariot burials, some of which have provided us with some of the finest artefacts to come from the ancient world. However, as beautiful and sophisticated as their artwork was, as Barry Raftery has said 'more important was their development for the first time of an effective ironworking industry in Europe'.

Around 450 BC, a new Celtic culture emerged after Hallstatt society declined because of reasons that are not completely clear. This was a time of great

*Triskele (bronze) shield mount found in Tal y Llyn (Meirionnydd)*

*Detail of La Tene decoration on a sword scabbard (bronze) found at Lisnacrogher Co. Antrim to*

Celtic expansion when tribes migrated across Europe and the period is known as La Tène, after the discovery of a major votive deposit of over 2000 artefacts in Lake Neuchâtel in Switzerland. For the most part the deposit consisted of weaponry and the most notable items were the fine swords, whose exquisitely decorated iron scabbards displayed a distinctive and complex curvilinear art, which characterises the La Tène period in many parts of Europe.

In recent years though, the Celts have come under attack from some quarters of academia. For example, Simon James and John Collis have argued that the Celts in Britain and Ireland are a 'modern' invention, brought about by the rise of 18th century nationalism and that the term 'Celtic' is not relevant to the two islands. Those who favour the 'anti-Celtic' stance, argued that no one in Britain or Ireland called themselves a 'Celt' before 1700 and that there were no Celtic invasions or migrations into the two islands, from the continent.

However, as Peter Berresford Ellis has suggested scholars such as James and Collis may have been 'more concerned with modern politics than the ancient Celtic civilisation'. This is perhaps a little unfair, but it is intriguing to note that such views were emerging at a time when devolution in Scotland and Wales, was a major concern of British politics.

Perhaps the last words on this hotly debated subject, are best left with Barry Raftery: '[t]he Celts settled across a vast area of Europe, and while the different groups never formed one politically unified society, they did share many aspects of material culture, language and religion. It is just this… that justifies the use of the term 'Celtic' as a convenient cultural label'.

It should perhaps be pointed out here that although the Iron Age in the British Isles is often seen to end with the invasion of the Romans in AD 43, for many people life would have carried on much the same as it had before Claudius and his legions arrived. It is true that in many parts of southern Britain the indigenous inhabitants were to a degree, 'Romanised', but in the northern and western fringes of the British Isles the Romans had less impact. The Romans never conquered Ireland and with Scotland, the Roman policy was one of containment rather than conquest as shown by the building of Hadrian's Wall and the Antonine Wall. Ultimately these barriers kept the Scottish Iron Age tribes (a Celtic people known as the Picts) in check and nullified the threat to the rich Roman province of southern Britain. Although the Romans also had a firm grip on Wales, as shown by the legionary fortresses found at Segontium (Caernarfon) and Caerleon (Gwent) they never completely conquered the country (as in Scotland, the rugged nature of the Welsh countryside played its part in hindering Roman occupation). In fact the peninsula has revealed little sign of Roman activity, though it has been suggested that the Romans attacked one of its hillforts (the evidence for this will be discussed in the next chapter).

One of the earliest examples of the first use of iron in the British Isles comes from the Llyn Fawr hoard in Glamorgan. A ritual or 'votive' deposit was made in the lake around 750 BC and as we have seen in Chapter 5, the practice of deliberately placing objects in watery places had a long heritage stretching back at least a far as the Neolithic. One of the best known Iron Age votive deposits in the British Isles was found at Llyn Cerrig Bach on Ynys Môn and this will also be discussed below.

Included among a number of bronze items deliberately

deposited in the lake was a fine iron sword of the 'Hallstatt' type (which were common on the continent) and an iron spearhead and socketed sickle. However, it would not be until c. 500 BC that iron fully replaced bronze as the metal used to make the everyday tools and weapons of the Early Iron Age communities spread across Europe. Although bronze did not disappear during the Iron Age, it was mainly used to make the ritual and ceremonial items used by the élite's of the time.

Linguistic evidence also provides us with further evidence of the veneration of water by the Iron Age communities of the British Isles. For example, the River Boyne in Ireland takes its name from the Celtic goddess Boann, while the river Glen in Lincolnshire derives its name from the British Celtic root, glanos, which means 'clean, holy, beautiful' (*glân* in modern Welsh). It is also possible that the River Alun in Flintshire takes its name from an ancient Celtic goddess who was known as Alaunae or Alounae among the Celts of ancient Gaul.

Iron differed from Bronze because furnaces could not reach the temperature that was required to completely melt iron ore into molten iron. The liquid bronze that resulted from the heating of the combination of copper, tin and lead ores could be poured straight into the stone moulds from which various objects were made. However, when iron ore was first heated in a furnace it produced an unusable 'bloom', which consisted of a mixture of iron and impurities from the ore (the slag). This bloom then had to undergo repeated heated and hammering by smiths until the slag was removed and a rectangular 'billet' of iron was formed. Finally, these billets were then heated again by smiths and worked into long thin bars of iron, ready to be transformed into the many different objects used by Iron Age communities.

Although bronze was still a useful material, iron did have some advantages over it and this is probably why it became the common metal in the latter half of the first millennium BC. Iron is not only a strong and durable material but it is also more flexible than bronze and thus new artefacts not seen before could be made. Iron ores are also more widely available than the copper, tin and lead needed to make bronze and in the British Isles they occur not only in wet bogs, but also on the surface.

Slag from iron production has been found on many Iron Age sites across the British Isles showing that ironworking was a common activity. Iron working sites have been identified at Bryn y Castell and Crawcwellt in Meirionnydd and the evidence found here has been very informative in regards to the ironworking process.

Large timber or stone buildings at these sites were used in iron production and they could contain up to fifteen low 'shaft furnaces'. Also found were large dumps of slag, hearth bases and smithing 'scale', which was waste from the production of iron billets and bars. Stone anvils used by smiths to make iron objects were also discovered.

At Llwyn Bryn-Dinas in Montgomeryshire, unusual evidence of both bronze and ironworking was discovered within the hillfort. The remains of a small, circular building were found and inside was a spread of smithing scale, lumps of slag and fragments of crucibles and furnace lining. Local copper was also used in the production of bronze at the site. It is evident that Iron Age smiths were extremely competent artisans who produced not only practical objects for use in daily life, but also objects used in conspicuous displays of wealth by those who occupied the upper echelons of Iron Age society. Practical objects included tools such as sickles for harvesting, and files, tongs and hammers used by blacksmiths, the design of which has changed little in over two thousand years. Shears used for both personal grooming and for the shearing of sheep have also been found. In Wales, tools from the Iron Age are very rare, and this must indicate that many were recycled for other uses.

The many weapons produced during the Iron Age remind us that it was a dangerous and volatile time and it is probable that the spears and javelins produced during this time would have been used more often in warfare than hunting. The common man in Iron Age society would have used spears and javelins whereas the 'aristocratic' warrior class would have favoured swords. These were often finely made and much time and effort went into their production.

*Castell Odo (85)*

*Castell Odo (86)*

*Castell Odo (87)*

*Aberdaron from Castell Odo (88)*

*Quern and rubbing stone (88a)*

*Late Bronze Age pottery found at Castell Odo (88b)*

*Bryn y Meillion (89)*

*Dinas Dinlle (90)*

*Dinas Dinlle (91)*

*Dinas Dinlle (92)*

*Pen y Gaer (93)*

*View from Pen y Gaer (94)*

*Pen y Gaer (95)*

*Porth Dinllaen (96)*

*Pared Mawr (97)*

*Pared Mawr (98)*

*Mynydd y Graig (99)*

*Plas Glyn y Weddw (100)*

*Plas Glyn y Weddw (101)*

*St Hywyn (102)*          *Llangian (103)*

*Llanaelhaearn (104)*

*St Aelhaearn (105)*        *Llannor (107)*

*Unmarked stone slab Llanaelhaearn (106)*

*Llangybi (108)*          *Clynnog (110)*

*Capel Uchaf (109)*

*Ffynnon Gybi (111-114)*

*Ffynnon Aelrhiw (115,116)*

*Ffynnon Saint near Rhiw (117)*

*Ffynnon Beuno (118)*

*Ffynnon Beuno (119)*

*Ffynnon Aelhaearn (120)*

*Ffynnon Fair, Bryncroes (121)*

*Ffynnon Fair, Bryncroes (122)*

*Ffynnon Grasi (123)*

*Ffynnon Felin Fach (124)*

Scabbards were often intricately decorated and red glass, horn, antler and coral were inlaid into hilts and scabbards to further enhance the finery of the swords. Unfortunately, Iron Age swords are also very rare in Wales, although as seen above, an example was found at Llyn Fawr and swords were found in the votive deposit at Llyn Cerrig Bach.

As in the preceding Neolithic and Bronze Age, religion was an important aspect of Iron Age life and a fair amount of fascinating archaeological evidence relating to the religious ceremonies and rituals carried out by the Iron Age people of the British Isles has been discovered. We have already come across some of this evidence with the Llyn Fawr votive deposit and as we saw, this also provided important evidence for the first appearance of iron in the British Isles. However, the Llyn Cerrig Bach votive deposit stands out as being perhaps the finest example of its kind in the British Isles.

The deposit was found in the small lake known as Llyn Cerrig Bach in 1943, when the nearby RAF airfield was being constructed. It consisted of a large amount of fine and varied metalwork that began to be deposited in the third century BC, or earlier, with continuing deposition up until AD 60, when the Romans invaded Anglesey. For the most part, the metalwork consisted of items that could be considered to be militaristic in character and amongst the many artefacts discovered (about 200) were a number of swords that had been deliberately bent or 'ritually killed' before being placed in the water. This 'ritual killing' of swords has also been noted in Celtic burials on the continent and it also appears that in other prehistoric periods various objects received similar treatment. For example, things such as axes, pots and arrowheads were deliberately broken before being placed in the ditches of the Neolithic, causewayed enclosure at Windmill Hill in Wiltshire. Arrowheads with their tips deliberately snapped off are also found in the burial chambers of Neolithic tombs and with the bodies placed under the burial mounds of the Early Bronze Age. Some of the archer's wristguards or bracers found in Beaker burials were also deliberately broken before being placed with the deceased. It does seems probable as Aubrey Burl has suggested, that this ritual behaviour reveals how prehistoric people believed that objects had to be 'killed' so that they could be used by the dead in the spirit world.

Also found were chariot and harness fittings, blacksmiths' tools, iron 'currency bars' used in trading, a bronze trumpet and interestingly, what appear to be slave chains. These last items fit with the notion that during the Iron Age warriors undertook raids on settlements in order to capture slaves who formed a lower class in Iron Age society. Similar slave chains have also been found in Hertfordshire and Cambridgeshire.

Many other fine items of metalwork which must represent Iron Age votive deposits have been found elsewhere in the British Isles and include the superbly decorated bronze shields found in the Thames near Battersea and in the River Witham in Lincolnshire, which are masterpieces of La Tène art. Being made of bronze, these artefacts would have been easily damaged if actually used in warfare and thus must have been designed as ceremonial items that were ritually deposited by wealthy Iron Age élite.

It is evident that Iron Age people also made votive deposits in deep shafts in the ground, which provide further tantalising reminders of their religious beliefs. For example at Ewell in Surrey, eight shafts which varied between four and twelve metres were discovered. Many different objects were found in these shafts and included the skeleton of a decapitated dog, iron nails, apple pips, cherry stones, an iron hammer and oyster shells. At Ashill in Norfolk a bewildering array of objects was found and appeared to represent a series of distinct deposits. At the bottom of the shaft the haunch bone of a deer had been laid on a bed of carefully arranged flints, while above these in the middle layers, pieces of antlers, a boar's tusk and pottery vessels were laid on beds of hazel and oak leaves. At the top of the shaft, there was a wicker basket, oxen and deer bones and below these mussel and oyster shells.

There are also hints that some pits may have contained human sacrifices. In a shaft in Bavaria a wooden pole was found in association with decomposed human flesh and traces of blood. Such evidence does not prove that a sacrificial victim was placed in this shaft, but evidence from widespread areas of Europe reveals that human sacrifices were deliberately deposited in watery places during the Iron Age.

One of the most famous examples of an Iron Age, Celtic sacrifice was found in August 1984, when a peat worker cutting peat at Lindow Moss in Cheshire discovered a human foot. Subsequent archaeological investigation of the area where the foot was found revealed the flattened but well preserved remains (his neatly trimmed moustache and beard could still be clearly seen) of a young man aged around 25 years old. It is thought that he was buried in the early years of the first century AD. Apart from a band of fox fur on his upper arm he was naked at the time of his burial and it seems that his death had not been a peaceful one. When the body was examined in the laboratory it was discovered that not only had his throat been cut but, he had also been strangled and had received violent blows to his skull.

While I was writing this book, further recent evidence for the Celtic practice of making sacrificial, votive deposits in watery places was reported in the press and on television. This evidence consisted of two male bodies from the Iron Age (dated to c. 300 BC) found in peat bogs (just 25 miles apart) in the summer of 2003, in County Offally, central Ireland. One of the men had been decapitated and had also had his legs cut off. It is possible that he was also tortured, as lengths of withy hurdles had been driven through his arms. The size of his arms and hands indicated that he had been a big man, unlike the other victim, who only appears to have been about 5.2 ft. Interestingly, the smaller man had sculpted his hair with pine resin (found only in south-west France or Spain) so that it stuck up from his head, which may reveal that he was self-conscious about his height. He too, had been murdered and it was evident that he had suffered vicious and fatal blows to his head that had left a gaping wound in his skull, through which his brain was still visible. His throat was also probably cut and his forearms, hands and legs had also been cut off.

The archaeologists that featured on the BBC 2

'Timewatch' programme about the discovery of the two bodies put forward some fascinating theories regarding the sacrificial victims. Ned Kelly suggested that 'Clonycavan Man' and 'Croghan Man' (the names of the peat bogs in which the victims were found) were offerings to gods of fertility and placed on tribal boundaries in order to ensure the continuation of the kingship and tribe and the fertility of crops and animals. Timothy Taylor followed a different line of reasoning, suggesting that Iron Age bog bodies represent criminals who were placed in a 'liminal' world that was neither of the living or the dead and thus their souls were trapped in limbo.

A number of other Iron Age 'bog bodies' have also been discovered in bogs and marshes across northern Europe and many of these also seem to represent ritual sacrifices placed in lakes or pools. For example, the famous 'Tollund Man' found in a peat bog in Denmark had a rope around his neck, which had almost certainly been used to hang him. Another male bog body found at Grauballe about 11 miles away from Tollund Man also appears to have been ritually killed, as his throat had been cut from ear to ear.

Of course the bog bodies could be interpreted as evidence of violent acts such as revenge killings or the execution of criminals, but the theory of ritual sacrifice perhaps holds more weight (though some of the people who were sacrificed may well have been people who had seriously transgressed against Iron Age society), however horrific it seems to us today. Further support for this theory is provided by the classical authors and for example, Lucan, writing in the first century AD tells us of a sacred, Celtic grove near Marseilles where 'the altars were heaped with hideous offerings, and every tree was sprinkled with human gore'. He also refers to the sacrifices made to the Celtic gods Teutates, Esus and Taranis, by the continental Celtic tribes known as the Treveri and Ligurians. Also, Strabo and Caesar both provide accounts of the Celtic practice of building huge wooden figures into which both animals and humans were burnt alive in honour of the gods (made famous in the film The Wicker man).

Admittedly, the above classical accounts of Celtic

sacrifices were undoubtedly biased towards a Roman audience and were used as a form of anti-Celtic propaganda, but as we have seen above, the archaeological evidence proves that the Iron Age Celts did make sacrifices. We should not lose sight of the fact that human sacrifice was certainly not unknown in many other ancient and 'primitive' societies. For example, the fabulously preserved mummies of young children found in graves on high snow-covered peaks in the Andes, were sacrificial victims dedicated to Inca gods over five hundred years ago. In Ecuador, the flesh from human sacrifices was scattered on fields in tribal fertility rituals, while the Pawnee Indians are known to have sacrificed young girls in their 'Morning Star ceremony'.

It may well be that the famous Celtic 'Druids', instigated the sacrifices made during the Iron Age. Indeed Strabo tells us '[t]hey offered their sacrifices not without a druid', while Caesar tells us in his De Bello Gallico that the Druids 'regulate public and private sacrifices'. However, while it is clear that the druids played an important part in Celtic religious practices, it is probably better to see them as an intellectual class rather than an all-powerful priesthood. Caesar tells us that the Druids were 'an intellectual class' and Strabo informs us that 'the Druids, in addition to the science of nature, study also moral philosophy.' As Peter Berresford Ellis tells us 'Celtic society was based on a caste system and that the second level was the intellectual class. This class encompassed all the professional occupations – judges, doctors, historians and genealogists, philosophers, storytellers, astronomers and astrologers, as well as the priestly orders who mediated with the deities'. Of course, the writings of classical authors reflect the outlook of the society of which they were part, and so, we cannot totally accept them at face value. Whatever the reality of the druids, we will leave them now as we turn to take a brief look at the more prosaic aspects of Iron Age life in the peninsula.

The people who lived in the peninsula during the Early Iron Age would have had to contend with a climate that had been deteriorating since about 1200 BC and it was cold and wet until around 400 BC, when relatively warm and dry conditions returned. The woodlands of the peninsula had begun to be cleared as early as the Neolithic period, but it was not until the Iron Age that extensive clearances which would really leave their mark on the landscape, began to take place.

As is the case with the other prehistoric peoples we have already discussed in this book, the communities of the Iron Age would not have had the benefits of modern medicine, healthcare and a balanced diet. Not surprisingly therefore, their lifespan was short and skeletons found at Iron Age sites confirm this. The Iron Age cemetery near Deal in Kent (Mill Hill) is more well known for the fine warrior burial that was found there, but study of other skeletons from the cemetery revealed that few adults would have survived beyond fifty years and that child-birth must have killed many young women. At the famous Danebury hillfort in Hampshire, study of the skeletons found buried in pits within the defences showed that a quarter of children did not make it to the age of two and that people generally suffered from poor health. It is also clear that like their predecessors in the Neolithic and Bronze Age, the people of the Iron Age were seriously affected by arthritis of the spine brought on by the rigours of a strenuous lifestyle. Undoubtedly, the Iron Age people of the peninsula faced the same hardships as their counterparts elsewhere in the British Isles, though we should remember that although life for many prehistoric people would have often been hard and brief, it must also have held its pleasures too.

In Chapter 8 we will look at the hillforts of the peninsula which have to be the most distinctive feature of the Iron Age in the British Isles and Europe. Before this however, we will briefly examine the other forms of settlement that would have existed here in the Iron Age and the methods of farming also.

There seems to have been a fair amount of variation amongst the 'non-hillfort' settlements that were built in Wales during the Iron Age, though as Frances Lynch has noted 'the dominant settlement in later prehistoric times was the lightly enclosed or open farmstead'. These farmsteads would contain one or more roundhouses, with wooden and stone walls, or walls of wattle work covered with clay and surrounded by slight banks and ditches. Not surprisingly it is the stone round-houses that have stood the test of time, though aerial photography has helped greatly in identifying the former existence of wooden round-houses which now appear as crop-marks in the landscape. A number of stone round-houses still survive in the landscape of the peninsula and although there is some uncertainty to their date because of a lack of excavation, many are likely to date to the Iron Age.

However, firm evidence of two Iron Age farming settlements has been found on the Graeanog Ridge on the eastern edge of the peninsula. At both Graeanog (c. 175 BC-75 AD) and Cefn Graeanog II (c. 200-150 BC), excavations uncovered the remains of stone roundhouses and the latter site was also associated with a prehistoric field system. It is likely that these stone roundhouses replaced earlier timber buildings as evidence for farming activity dating to 410-215 BC, was found on the ridge. Artefacts found at the settlements also revealed that the farms had continued to be occupied into the Romano-British period.

Some non-hillfort settlements of the Iron Age in Wales do seem to have been built with defence in mind and many examples of fortified settlements have been found in south-west Wales. For example, near Llawhaden in Pembrokeshire a group of three, defended enclosures were excavated at Drim, Woodside and Dan y Coed. Although not particularly large (the diameter of each enclosure measured some 40m), these sites were fortified with substantial ditches and banks and at Drim and Woodside, wooden watch-towers were situated at the entrances to the settlements.

The farms of the Iron Age would have practised mixed agriculture with the rearing of both crops and animals and although the picture of Iron Age subsistence in Wales is not completely clear emphasis may have been on a pastoral economy. Nevertheless, the growing of cereals was still an important feature of farming in Iron Age Wales and while the best preserved fields of this time are found at sites along the northern and western edges of Snowdonia (such as Graeanog), fine examples are found elsewhere (e.g. on Skomer Island).

Arable farming in Iron Age Wales is also attested by the rare examples of plough-marks found at sites such as Drim and Woodbarn Rath. Unfortunately, the ploughs used in arable farming are even rarer, though the tip of a wooden plough or ard was discovered at Walesland Rath in Pembrokeshire.

As to the crops grown on Iron Age farms in Wales, it is clear that as in other parts of the British Isles, wheat and barley were commonly grown staples with both spelt and emmer wheat grown. The stone querns and mortars which were used for processing cereals have been found on many sites in Wales, and are particularly common in north-western Wales, revealing that the growing of crops in this region was an integral aspect of Iron Age subsistence.

Unfortunately, because of the acidic nature of the soils in many parts of Wales, the evidence for the animals kept on Iron Age farms is scarce. Nevertheless, at Goldcliff West in the Gwent Levels there was a remarkable survival of cattle hoofprints close to the unusually well preserved remains of wooden buildings which probably belonged to a seasonal grazing camp dating to the fourth century BC. At the Early/Middle Iron Age settlement of Bryn Eryr on Anglesey, cattle and sheep were present, while at Coygan Camp (Carmarthenshire) and Dinorben (Denbighshire); cattle and sheep were the dominant animals, respectively. Pigs, goats and domestic fowl were also kept and the hunting and fishing of wild game further supplemented the diets of Iron Age communities in Wales.

## Chapter 9

# Hillforts

Hillforts are the most instantly recognisable sites of the Iron Age and they survive in their thousands in the British Isles and on the continent. In his brief but very useful *Hillforts in England and Wales*, James Dyer defines a hillfort as 'a deliberately constructed fortification, built of earth, timber or stone, usually situated in an easily defended position, and frequently on a hilltop'. The word *hillfort* is sometimes used misleadingly, as it is apparent that not all sites were located on hills and some do not seem to have been constructed with defence in mind. Nevertheless, it would be fair to say that many hillforts do match the criteria outlined by Dyer and it is obvious that defence was a prime concern of their builders.

There is considerable variation in the size of hillforts and some enclose areas under 1 hectare, while at the other end of the scale, they can reach to over 80 hectares. However, Many hillforts are between 1.2 and 12 hectares in size and the defences normally consist of one or more ramparts or banks, with a deep outer ditch in front.

Hillforts that consist of only one rampart and ditch are known as *univallate*, while those featuring two or more defensive circuits, are known as *multivallate*. Ramparts were made from combinations of stone, timber and earth and many would have been capped by walkways and palisades, which would have been used by sentries or by the defenders of hillforts that were under attack. In western parts of the British Isles, there are several forts whose defences consist only of stone walls (no doubt dictated by the local geography), and examples of these walled forts can still be seen in the peninsula.

Wales is particularly well represented in terms of hillforts and there is a dense cluster of sites found in the south-west of the country. However, significant numbers of hillforts still survive in other parts of the country and in the peninsula there is a notable concentration of hillforts, which includes some superb examples of these characteristic and often impressive, Iron Age sites.

Although not large in number, fortified hilltop settlements in the British Isles were first built during the Neolithic and Carn Brea (Cornwall) and Crickley Hill (Gloucestershire) stand out as fine examples. During the Late Bronze Age (c. 1000 BC), fortifications were also built around hilltop settlements such as Norton Fitzwarren (Somerset) and Rams Hill (Berkshire). However, it was not until the Late Bronze Age/Early Iron Age transition (c.800-550 BC) that we see the true emergence of the hillfort phenomenon, which was to leave such a distinctive mark on the landscape of the British Isles.

The most common form of defence in these early hillforts was a single, wooden palisade and these have been detected below the later Iron Age defences of several hillforts in Wales. At Dinorben (Flintshire) for example, a series of palisades was recognised below a later rampart, which dated to around the fifth century BC and it is likely that these palisades were built between the ninth and seventh centuries BC. Other examples of probable Late Bronze Age palisades below later Iron Age forts include the Pembrokeshire forts of Dale and the well known Castell Henllys. As will be seen below, the origins of Castell Odo hillfort in Llŷn seem to lie in the Late Bronze Age and one wonders how many other of the peninsula's hillforts originated in this period? It is quite possible that traces of Late Bronze Age palisades still exist below the later defences of some of the peninsula's hillforts, but unfortunately, these will probably never be revealed.

As hillforts passed into a more developed stage in the Iron Age proper, box ramparts replaced the palisades of the early period of hillfort building. Box ramparts varied in their design, but essentially, they comprised a double line of posts, which were linked together with a series of horizontal posts that formed a wooden framework or box. Soil, stones or chalk (or a combination of these materials) would then be piled into this framework and a rampart walk and wooden breastwork must then have been added. An excavated example of a box rampart from Wales, sheds more light on the various techniques employed in their construction.

This was found at the well known hillfort of Moel y Gaer (located among the beautiful hills of the Clwydian Range in northern Wales), where excavations revealed the postholes of a rampart built during the early history of the site. When complete, the rampart had consisted of three parallel rows of posts, with the uprights of the outer rows being set close together (at intervals of under a metre) and the spaces between them filled with drystone walling. The posts were linked with horizontal 'lacing' timbers and between the inner and outer row there was a central row of larger posts that probably acted as an overall supporting device for the rampart and stopped the outer face from collapsing. The excavations also showed that hurdling had probably been used to divide the rampart up into a number of boxes or cells, which contained the soil that formed the main bulk of the rampart.

It is also evident from the design of hillfort entrances that there were various types and that some must have been designed as an additional defensive measure. For example, at Chun Castle in Cornwall, there is a good example of a 'staggered' entrance, common in many *multivallate* hillforts. Many of these entrances seem to have been designed so that people entering hillforts were 'channelled' left into passages and thus generally, any attackers would leave their undefended sword side vulnerable to attack from the ramparts above. Several hillforts also contain what are known as 'inturned' entrances and these were basically long passages leading into forts, which featured gates at either end and in some cases, what appear to be guard chambers situated nearby. A good Welsh example is provided by Castell Henllys, where there was a long passage which ended in a set of gates overlooked by a timber tower. Behind the gates, were two pairs of small rooms that were probably guard-chambers, which have been noted at other Welsh hillforts such as Dinorben and Moel Hiraddug (Flintshire).

Some entrances were more elaborate and featured long passages, turns leading to dead ends, and outworks in front of gateways, which resembled the barbicans seen in medieval forts. At the Iron Age fort on Crickley Hill, there was a bank with a gate at the end of it, which curved out from the main rampart to form a hornwork that any attackers would have had to pass under. Similar thought seems to have gone into the defences at Danebury, where a 'command post' was probably situated on the hornwork that stood in the centre of the entrance complex. This hornwork was located in a position that controlled two gates and looked out over a large portion of the fort's ditches and outer ramparts. Any attacking force would thus have been very vulnerable if they tried to storm this part of the hillfort.

Both excavation and visible remains have provided us with evidence of what the interiors of hillforts originally looked like and of the various activities that took place inside them. It is now realised that there was considerable variation in the way in which hillfort interiors were organised, with some featuring carefully arranged rows or 'streets', while in others, houses were arranged haphazardly.

Houses within the hillforts were generally round (though rectangular and square houses are known) and could be made from either wood or stone. During the Iron Age (and Bronze Age), stone houses were favoured in western parts of the British Isles because of the rocky nature of the landscape and the foundations of these can still be seen in many hillforts. Indeed as we will see, the remains of hundreds of stone roundhouses can be seen in the major hillforts of the peninsula. It seems that the timbers that supported the roofs of stone roundhouses rested on the tops of their walls, as they seldom reach over 2m in height. In some cases, stone porches were also added to provide protection from the elements.

The wooden roundhouses seem to have had outer walls consisting of either wooden posts laid in a continuous wall slot, or walls made from wattle and daub (or a combination of the two). In the larger examples, an inner ring of posts provided support for the roof. One of the great mysteries of the Iron Age is what the roofs of roundhouses actually looked like, but it seems highly likely that they were conical in fashion and for the most part resembled the roofs on the modern reconstructions of Iron Age houses that we see today. Such houses can be seen in Wales at places such as Castell Henllys and the museum of Welsh Life at Saint

Fagan's, where fascinating insights into Iron Age life are provided by impressive reconstructions of Iron Age settlements. It is also possible that some of the less sturdy roundhouses with wattle-work walls, had beehive-shaped roofs. Roofs in both the stone and wooden roundhouses must have consisted of either thatch, reeds or turf.

The floors of the roundhouses were made from flattened chalk or clay, or in some cases, stone paving and must have been covered with straw, reeds, and perhaps as James Dyer has suggested, herbs were also strewn on floors. It also seems likely that roundhouses featured internal screens that marked off sleeping quarters and there may even have been upper platforms where children slept.

Although evidence of crafts such as weaving and metalworking has often been found within roundhouses during excavations, it is hard to distinguish 'commercial' from domestic activity. It does seem probable however, that some roundhouses functioned solely as workshops where such things as metalworking and weaving took place.

In many hillforts, excavations have uncovered evidence of rectangular four-post structures, which seem to have been granaries, though they could have had other purposes such as containers for storing hay. Evidence that these small structures were used for storing grain has been found at Crickley Hill, where barley was preserved in two 'four-posters' that had burnt down. At Croft Ambrey (Herefordshire), there appears to have been hundreds of four-posters and as James Dyer has suggested, this implies that the site could store huge quantities of grain. Four-posters have also been found at a number of Welsh hillforts such as Dinorben, Ffridd Faldwyn and Moel y Gaer.

Also frequently found during hillfort excavations are pits lined with clay, stone or wickerwork, which were used for the storage of grain and perhaps other foodstuffs. Archaeology has revealed that fires were sometimes lit in pits, which must have been done in order to dry the walls and kill off bacteria. Once redundant, storage pits seem to have been used as both rubbish dumps and toilets, and these pits, after being sealed with clay or dung, were effective for several months. It should also be pointed out here, that it is probable that some of the presumed 'rubbish dumps' actually represent votive deposits made by Iron Age people. There also appears to be some evidence for religious structures within hillfort interiors, which is perhaps not surprising considering the religious significance of hilltops to prehistoric people. For example, at Maiden Castle, a circular stone building lay at the end of the main road that ran from the eastern gate. This structure lay next to a later Romano-Celtic temple, which strongly indicates that it too had a religious function of some sort. At the famous hillfort of South Cadbury in Somerset, which is associated with King Arthur, even firmer evidence for the existence of a temple was uncovered. This consisted of a square structure with a porch (built around AD 43), that was approached by a road on either side of which, animals and weapons were buried.

Human burials have also been found in hillforts in both storage pits and their surrounding ditches and we cannot escape the gruesome but distinct possibility that some of these burials were 'dedicatory', sacrificial burials made in honour of the gods. It is also seems that some burials represent the victims of warfare that took place at hillforts in both the Iron Age and the Romano-British period and we will look at these in more detail below.

**Hillforts of the peninsula**
The hillforts of the peninsula can basically be divided into two types – *Contour forts and Promontory forts.* The former which are considered to be the classic forts of the Iron Age are often located on prominent hilltops and as their name suggests, their ramparts follow the contours of hilltops. Contour forts were not always placed on significant hills, as shown by the magnificent Maiden Castle in Dorset, which is located on a contour that only rises to some 25m above the surrounding land.

Promontory forts rely to a large extent on natural defences around their perimeters and they are found on spurs of land either on coastal margins or above inland river valleys. In particular, these types of hillforts are found in large numbers along the coasts of south-western England and Wales, though they are also found in some numbers on

Ynys Môn.

Before we proceed to examine the peninsula's hillforts, it should also be mentioned that a few of the sites included in the following survey of the peninsula's hillforts might actually be later in date than the Iron Age. It is quite probable that additional defences were added to some of the peninsula's forts around the time of the Roman conquest and reveal the native response to the threat of attack by the Roman legionaries. It is also quite possible that some were built in the post-Roman period, or 'Dark Ages', as this time is more commonly known. During this time, the Saxon threat loomed ever larger on the horizon and Irish raiders were also attacking Wales. Also, the power vacuum left by the final withdrawal of the Roman legions in the early fifth century, meant that native warlords began to grapple for control in Wales. It is worth mentioning here that there is probably a small Dark Age fort located on the summit of Garn Boduan in Llŷn.

However, it does not really matter if we are unsure about the dates of some of the peninsula's hillforts, because whether they belong to the Iron Age or the Dark Ages, they are ancient places, which bring us closer to the people who lived here. In any case, it is perhaps worth pointing out, that the Dark Age inhabitants of the peninsula were to all intents and purposes still living an Iron Age lifestyle.

### Tre'r Ceiri (63, 64, 65, 66, 67, 68, 69)

Tre'r Ceiri ('town of the giants') is undoubtedly the jewel in the crown amongst the peninsula's hillforts and it survives in a remarkable state of preservation. Visiting Tre'r Ceiri is almost like walking back in time and Michael Senior in his *Hillforts of northern Wales*, nicely captures the atmosphere that still pervades this haunting place: 'Tre'r Ceiri is much as its inhabitants left it... You feel their presence around you. You feel almost embarrassed to be there, as if you have wandered into their town while they were out, and at any moment they may come back.'

The fort is located on the summit of the most easterly peak of Yr Eifl, which rises to around 1500 ft and offers magnificent all-round views of the peninsula and beyond.

This is a must-see site for those intending to visit the ancient sites and monuments of the peninsula and without doubt, is one of the finest ancient sites in the British Isles.

The superbly preserved remains at Tre'r Ceiri provide us with an unrivalled picture of what a large Welsh hillfort would actually have looked like in its original state. A hugely impressive stone wall still encloses the hilltop and on the north-west it still reaches around 13 ft high and 10-15 ft in width. On top of this stretch of wall there is a parapet and wall walk which would have provided sentries with an early warning of any approaching trouble and would have been a good platform for launching sling stones and other missiles. This massive stone wall represents the earliest phase of defence at the site and although we have no conclusive evidence for this, it seems probable that it dates to the later part of the Iron Age.

The remains of a large, outer wall can also still be seen on the north-western side of the mountain (the weakest side of the fort from a defensive viewpoint) and it is probable that this outer rampart is later in date than the inner wall. Other fragmentary remains of stone walls can still be seen in many places outside the inner rampart, but it is not clear what their original function was. However, A. Hogg who excvated the site in 1956 suggests in his 1960 report, that they probably represent livestock enclosures and possible garden plots (though growing conditions cannot have been particularly favourable!).

There appear to have been a number of entrances at Tre'r Ceiri, with the major ones at the south-western and western sides of the fort. These entrances appear to have consisted of stone walled passages measuring around 18 ft and 15 ft long, respectively. It is also apparent that there were three smaller gateways or 'posterns' in the original enclosure of the fort and the furthest one on the north still survives with is lintel intact. There cannot be many other such intact gates to be found among the many hillforts of the British Isles.

Within the wall were the remains of around one hundred and fifty dwellings, which vary considerably in their form and circular, D-shaped, pear-shaped, irregular, rectangular and square examples can be seen. Hogg arranged these structures typologically and suggested that the earliest buildings were the simple circular ones and the latest, the irregular and rectangular examples. Some support for his scheme of typological development is perhaps provided by the fact that large amounts of Roman period pottery were found in the rectangular huts.

It should also be mentioned that it is probable that not all the structures were actually dwellings and it seems likely that some functioned as workshops or storage areas and this could be suggested by the small size of some of the buildings.

Over the years Tre'r Ceiri has undoubtedly seen a fair number of 'non-scientific' excavations, which may well account for the general scarcity of finds at the site. Nevertheless, a number of serious archaeological investigations have been carried out at the hillfort and Rev. S. Baring-Gould and Robert Burnard carried out the first of these in 1904. Although their methods of excavation would be somewhat frowned upon by modern archaeologists, they nevertheless discovered some interesting and notable artefacts at the site and these are invaluable reminders of the people who once lived in this magnificent hillfort.

Their excavations were concentrated on the 'cytiau' (huts) and they dug down into the subsoil of some of these 'so as to make sure that domestic objects had not found their way between the rude paving stones, down to and beyond the stone packing'. Among the domestic objects they found were a few spindle whorls, an iron adze-hammer, an iron bill-hook various pottery sherds (belonging to Roman period vessels) and the remains of a nice bone comb that had been ornamented with iron pins.

The most notable finds were the gold plated bronze 'fibula' or brooch, and two intriguing beads. The excavators say of these small but notable artefacts: 'The two porcelain beads are of Egyptian manufacture. One of them we are informed, is the finest that has been found and recorded in the United Kingdom, and by its shape, paste, and glaze reveals its origin as either Alexandria or the Basin of the Nile'. The colour illustrations of the beads that appear in the report by Baring-Gould and Burnard (*Archaeologia*

*Cambrensis* 1904), suggest that the beads may well be made of faience. The fibula is decorated in the typical La Tène style of the later Iron Age, but probably dates to the Roman period. The significance of these finds will be discussed below.

Shortly after Baring-Gould's and Burnard's excavations in 1904, further excavations were directed at Tre'r Ceiri by Harold Hughes in 1906. Again, a varied and interesting collection of artefacts was discovered and he also appears to have found evidence of burials outside the fort. Among the artefacts relating to domestic activity were various pieces of broken pottery (again, Roman in date), several 'pot-boilers' (heated stones used for boiling water), a probable iron ladle, sheep, ox and horse bones, and stone 'rubbers' and pounders, which were probably used in food preparation.

The most significant finds were the corroded remains of a gold-plated 'beaded' torc made from bronze (a similar one was found not far from Clynnog Fawr in 1834), a gold-plated bronze pin and a 'pewter object' which was found in the additional excavation of two probable graves on a saddle below the hill. The exact function of this object is not clear, though the excavator feels that it may well be the pommel of a sword hilt, although it is also possible that it is a shield boss.

As mentioned above A.Hogg directed further excavations at Tre'r Ceiri in 1956, but although his work helped in an understanding of Tre'r Ceiri as a structure, he uncovered very little evidence of the people who lived here. As he disappointingly tells us of his excavation of Hut 28, '[a]mong the rubble were found some scraps of burnt bone and a small fragment of a shale ring, the only artifact discovered during the excavations'.

A walk to the summit of Tre'r Ceiri will bring you to the now badly ruined burial cairn mentioned in Chapter 6. Originally this would have been a significant feature of the site and may well have been revered as a sacred monument by the people who lived here.

### Garn Boduan *(70, 71, 72, 73)*

Although, not as well preserved as Tre'r Ceiri, this is still a very impressive site and should definitely be put on the itinerary of any one wishing to visit the hillforts of the peninsula. The hillfort lies about 1 mile south of Nefyn on a steep-sided and isolated hill that rises to about 900 ft. Within the defences, the remains of around 170 stone 'houses' (again, it seems probable that not all were dwellings) can be seen and interestingly, a look at the site plan shows that these all appear to be circular in shape. As we have seen at Tre'r Ceiri, there was great variation to be found among the structures here, though what the architectural homogeneity at Garn Boduan indicates is unclear.

As at Tre'r Ceiri, the hillfort defences were considerable and comprised of an inner and outer stone rampart, which are also thought to mark two separate phases of occupation at the site. Although the ramparts have now collapsed they would originally have been formidable barriers, with the earlier rampart measuring some 9-10 ft in width and the larger and later rampart some 13 ft. Although it is hard to ascertain the original height of the first rampart, like the second rampart, it was probably at least 6ft in height.

No entrance has been found in the earlier rampart, but there appear to have been two associated with the later one. The entrance on the south-east, by which one approaches the fort today, is now badly ruined but is likely to have been the main entrance into the fort when it was occupied. The entrance on the north-east is smaller and seems to have been blocked at some point in the ancient past.

A. Hogg was also responsible for the archaeological investigations that were made at Garn Boduan in May and June 1954 and as at Tre'r Ceiri, he was not particularly successful in uncovering evidence of the original occupants of the hillfort. The finds comprise of two sling stones, a flint flake and a number of finds from within and near the small, possible Dark Age fort which is located on the summit of the hill. These finds consisted of several ornamental beads, which could have been made any time between the first and seventh centuries AD, a fragment of Roman pottery (late first/early second century) and some possible sherds of Dark Age pottery. As dating evidence for the small fort, this was therefore rather inconclusive, but the name of the hill, which means the 'home of Buan', does suggest that it was occupied in the Dark Ages. Buan was a son of the sixth century prince, Llywarch Hen and he lived in the first half of the seventh century, though whether he actually lived at Garn Boduan is open to question.

### Garn Fadrun *(74, 75, 76, 77, 78)*

This is the third of the peninsula's major hillforts, but as far as I am aware, it has not been archaeologically investigated. It is situated only about 4 miles from Garn Boduan, which can easily be seen from the site (and vice versa), on a solitary peak that rises to around 1000 ft from the middle of Llŷn. Yet again, the views from this hillfort are breathtaking and wide-ranging and on a very clear day the Wicklow Hills are faintly discernible across the Irish Sea.

As with Tre'r Ceiri and Garn Boduan, we appear to have two separate phases of occupation at Garn Fadrun, which are marked by an inner rampart and a larger outer rampart. Traces of both these ramparts can still be seen at various points on the mountain and although their original dimensions are unknown, it seems probable that as at the above hillforts, they would have been of considerable size. The remains of many stone buildings can still be seen both within the ramparts and also outside them, with a notable cluster below the summit on the western side.

The entrances are badly ruined today, but it appears that there were two main entrances into the fort on its north-western and south-western sides, (which provides the main point of entry into the fort today). Traces of the stone walls that lined the passage of the north-western entrance can also still be seen.

Mention should also be made of the remains of a small fort that can also be seen on the summit of the mountain and it is extremely likely that this is a twelfth century fort that was mentioned by Giraldus Cambrensis in his *Itinerary*. The burial cairn that was mentioned in Chapter 6, lies opposite on an outcrop of rock that rises above the cluster of buildings mentioned above.

### Craig y Ddinas *(79, 80, 81)*

This is something of a hidden gem amongst the peninsula's

hillforts and is situated amongst some of the most beautiful countryside in the peninsula. Snowdon is also clearly visible from the site, and can be seen rising majestically to the north-east, framed by the mountains that mark the entrance to the Nantlle Valley. Craig y Ddinas is a classic promontory fort and is located on the flat top of a 200 ft promontory, about 1.5 miles from the village of Pontllyfni on the northern coast of the peninsula. On the eastern side of the fort, steep, thickly wooded slopes fall some 50 ft to the Afon Llyfni, which can be seen rushing by below.

The most striking features of this hillfort are the massive double ramparts and ditches that defend the fort's western side. The outer rampart still stands to a height of around 10ft and the inner rampart reaches to about 12ft. As you follow the ditch that runs below the inner rampart, the top of the rampart is some 14ft above you and you feel dwarfed by its size. Any attacking force that breached the first strong line of defence would therefore find itself facing an even more formidable barrier with the inner rampart.

Limited excavations in 1939, revealed that the inner rampart comprised of a 12 ft thick, composite wall that consisted of an inner filling of earth and stones and outer faces of small stone slabs. The excavators also suggested that the inner rampart may contain wooden architectural components, though without further excavation we cannot discover whether this is the case.

Although it is now badly ruined, traces of the stone wall that once surrounded the fort on the edge of the promontory, can still be seen and it is apparent that this was at least 10 ft thick, though its original height is not clear. There were two entrances, at either end of the inner rampart and although now blocked by fallen stones, they seem to have been straight passages about 12 ft in length.

Again, it is thought that the remains seen today represent two different periods of construction and thus two different periods of occupation. Unfortunately, finds have been scarce at Craig y Ddinas and it is therefore hard to put a date on the site, though it seems quite probable that the defences that we can still see today originated in the Late Iron Age. Whatever the reality behind the date, one thing is clear – its builders certainly seem to have been concerned with defending themselves.

Mention should also be made of the large grass-covered mound, which can be seen in the interior of the fort. While this is likely to be artificial and probably associated with the original occupation of Craig y Ddinas, it is hard to say what it represents.

### Garn Pentyrch *(82, 83, 84)*

This interesting hillfort crowns the summit of a hill that rises around 720 ft above the famous holy well at Llangybi (which will be discussed in the next chapter). There are still some fairly substantial remains to be seen and although it is somewhat hard to make sense of these today, there were three lines of defence. Although damaged by later farming activity, it is evident that the outer defence consists of an earthen bank and ditch on the north, which is replaced on the western half of its circuit by a large stone wall, which appears to have been at least 5 ft high, originally.

Likewise, the middle rampart comprises of a similar combination of earthen bank and ditch and stone rampart. These defences are fairly formidable, with the bank still reaching 9 ft in height and although the stone wall is now collapsed, it seems to have been 10-15 ft wide (though its width thickens to 30 ft at the obscured entrance passage to the east) and probably reached a similar height as the earthen rampart.

The inner stone rampart is quite well preserved and again, it is apparent that it would have been a very strong defensive feature, when complete. Although, it is now collapsed, it varies in width from 10-25 ft and still stands to around 5ft in places. Originally, it is likely to have been around 9 ft high or even higher. An account of the site in *Archaeologia Cambrensis* in 1873 mentions the existence of a parapet walk on the inner rampart, but unfortunately, this can no longer be seen.

The Royal Commission feels that the three lines of defence are 'probably not all of one period', but unfortunately no evidence has been found that could help in dating the site, though an Iron Age date for the earliest period seems likely.

**Castell Odo** *(85, 86, 87, 88, 88a, 88b)*
Not much remains today of this small hillfort, which is situated on a low hill (Mynydd Ystum, 480 ft) about 2 miles outside the pretty coastal village of Aberdaron which lies not far from the peninsula's end and Ynys Enlli. Nevertheless, traces of the double banks that once encircled this settlement can still be seen, particularly on the fort's western side and the scrubby and uneven interior hints at the existence of former buildings.

Castell Odo is an important site, as it has provided evidence of how the origins of many Iron Age hillforts lay in the Late Bronze Age. As is the norm with the peninsula's hillforts, the site is worth visiting purely for appreciating the beauty of its countryside and as Michael Senior has said of the site, 'it has the highly characteristic feature of a sublime and inspiring outlook'.

There have been two sets of archaeological excavations at Castell Odo and C.E. Breese carried out the first of these in 1929. During his excavations he investigated both the houses and the outer rampart and found hearths within four of the houses on the site. He also discovered flint tools, saddle querns, a stone pounder, around a dozen sling stones and a crude and simple pottery sherd. For many years after Breese's excavations at Castell Odo, it was felt that it was a classic Dark Age Site of the post-Roman period. This was because the piece of pot found by Breese shared some similarities to pottery found at a Dark Age site at Pant-y-Saer on Ynys Môn. However, as we will see below, it is now evident that the date of Castell Odo lies much further back in time.

Dr. Leslie Alcock, who investigated the site during two seasons of excavations in 1958 and 1959, directed the most significant excavations at Castell Odo. He uncovered the sequential development of the site and divided the history of Castell Odo into four main phases of occupation. According to Alcock, the earliest settlement appears to have consisted of 'an undefended village of wooden houses with thatch or turf roofs' and he discovered a stone drain associated with one of these houses as well as animal bones, teeth (probably belonging to cattle) and numerous pottery sherds. These sherds resembled the one found by Breese and likewise were not particularly exciting but as is often the way in archaeology, they were important because they gave a 'relative' date for the site. Although these insignificant pieces of pots have caused much heated debate amongst archaeologists over the years, as Frances Lynch has pointed out they 'are now recognised as later Bronze Age ceramics'. Thus the first phase of occupation at Castell Odo may have begun perhaps as early as c. 900 BC.

Also of some interest was Alcock's discovery of evidence that pointed strongly to an attack on the Late Bronze Age settlement on Castell Odo. Although it is likely that the site was abandoned for a short while after this attack, the site was reoccupied and continued to be lived in through the Iron Age and probably into the Roman period. Intriguingly, further evidence from Castell Odo points to a later attack on the site and it is possible that a Roman military force was behind this. We will look at the evidence for the two attacks on Castell Odo in more detail below.

Apart from the pottery found at Castell Odo, there were some other interesting artefacts found at the site. Among these were small numbers of slingstones, two saddle querns for grinding corn, rubbing and pounding stones, probable whetstones, a flint knife or scraper, a possible ornamented spindle whorl or pulley for a bow-drill and a broken jet or lignite ring. It is possible that this ring was originally a harness ring that had been part of horse gear.

Inconclusive evidence of metalworking was also found and this consisted of very small fragments of rock that contained iron ore and a possible fragment of a bowl-furnace in which iron ore may have been smelted.

### Bryn Meillion (89)

This small hillfort is located on the lower slopes of Mynydd Rhiw and although not much of the original fort remains today, it is still possible to make out traces of the original enclosure and a ruined stone wall can be clearly seen on the eastern side. The date of the fort is unknown, but it is probable that the remains represent what was a multi-phase site, with the first phase perhaps dating to the Iron Age.

### Dinas Dinlle *(90, 91, 92)*

This hillfort is situated on the western coast of the peninsula, on a rounded hill (100 ft) not far from its start at Bontnewydd and from here there are particularly fine views along the coast of Arfon to Yr Eifl. Like Craig y Ddinas, the double ramparts of this hillfort greatly impress with their size and once again you are struck by the fact that even when located on low hills, the hillforts of the peninsula would have been very strong defensively.

On the west, the hillfort appears to have crumbled into the sea, but it is probable that the two ramparts originally encircled the fort. On the south-western side of the fort some of the stones used in the building of the inner rampart can still be seen, lying in a collapsed heap.

In the fort's interior the remains of huts and enclosures are marked by its undulating surface and a large oval mound in the north-eastern corner may be a plundered burial mound. However, W.E. Griffiths, writing in the journal of the Caernarvonshire Historical Society (1949), felt that the mound could be the remains of a signal-tower built by the Romans at Dinas Dinlle. The fact that several Roman coins of the late third century have been found at Dinas Dinlle (said to have been found in the mound) and that the fort of Segontium at Caernarfon lies only about 5 miles away, lends some support to this idea.

Whether the fort saw earlier occupation is not known, but it seems likely that it originated in the Iron Age, or perhaps even earlier. As Michael Senior has pointed out, the site is actually mentioned in one of the stories of the famous Mabinogion *(Math son of Mathonwy)* and although the stories featured in the Mabinogion have been distorted by time, they nevertheless provide us with strong echoes of Celtic, Iron Age life. Therefore, if the Romans did indeed set up a signal-tower inside the fort, we have to ask what happened to its native inhabitants It may be that the Romans drove them out in a military action. It has to be said though, that no evidence for this has been found.

### Pen y Gaer *(93, 94, 95)*

This fairly modest hillfort is located in a rather wild and

isolated corner of the peninsula on the eastern edge of the uplands that climb above the coast of Arfon. Nevertheless, this is an area that has a sparse beauty that can be appreciated from the hillfort, which crowns a distinctive and solitary hill that rises to a considerable 1270 ft.

The fort appears to have been defended by single circuit of stone wall, which still survives in a good condition on the western side. It seems that the wall was around 15 ft thick and about 8ft in height and is also unusual in that it appears to have two distinct sections of walling with the back section slightly higher than the front, which can still be clearly seen today. However, whether this 'double wall' indicates two periods of occupation, is unclear. Around the eastern side of the fort, the slopes are very steep and rocky and would have provided a strong, natural defence. Therefore the wall on this side of the fort does not appear to have been as strongly built and the remains are slighter than on the west.

It is still possible to make out the entrance into the fort, which lies between the ramparts on the west and it appears to have been a passage measuring some 11 ft long and 7 ft wide.

Although not much can now be seen within the enclosure, it is still possible to make out the traces of terraced platforms, which the Royal Commission tells us were the locations for wooden huts.

The only possible dating evidence for the fort was a single pottery sherd, which has now unfortunately been lost, though again, a date in the Iron age is possible for the remains that survive today.

### Porth Dinllaen (96)
Sadly, there is hardly anything to be seen of this coastal promontory fort, as it has been severely damaged by the building of the road that runs across Nefyn golf course down to the picturesque harbour and village at Porth Dinllaen. However, it is still possible to make out traces of the bank and ditch on the western side.

Like Dinas Dinlle, the prime function of the fort may have been to guard against invasion by sea. We could also speculate that these forts were used as trading entrepots, as there must have been much 'mercantile' traffic passing up and down the coast in the Iron Age and Roman period, though, admittedly, there is no actual evidence of this

**Pared Mawr** *(97, 98)*
This coastal promontory fort would perhaps be better viewed as a 'defended homestead' rather than an actual hillfort, as it its small size indicates that it was probably only home to a couple of families (the enclosure is sub-rectangular in shape and measures about 30 m north-west and 24 m south-east). It is located in a little visited area of the peninsula on the steep cliffs above the lovely beach of Porth Ceiriad, which lies not far from the popular holiday resort of Abersoch in Llŷn.

A fairly substantial rampart can still be seen on the north-western landward side of the fort and although now grass-grown, this was originally a considerable stone wall. A dump of stones is plainly visible below the fort, and there may be some connection between this and the building of the rampart. Traces of a circular building area one also still visible within the enclosure.

As there appears to have been no serious excavations at Pared Mawr and no record of any stray finds made here, it is hard to put a date on the site. However, it is similar in its form and location to the numerous other small, coastal forts in Wales, which have been dated to the Iron Age.

**Mynydd y Graig** *(99)*
Nothing much now remains of this small fort, though traces of the stone wall that surrounded it can still be seen, with the best-preserved section to the north. The fort is situated on the summit of the headland of Mynydd y Graig and to the south-east, the ground falls steeply away to the cliffs above the western end of Porth Neigwl. To the north-west, a rock gully can be seen and this probably formed the original entrance to the fort. If you can, visit this fort on a clear day, as you will be rewarded with a stunning view of Porth Neigwl and the headland of Mynydd Cilan. Beyond this, you will see the mountains of mid and northern Wales and the coastline as far as Pembrokeshire.

## The role of hillforts

Today, hillforts lie quiet, their ditches, banks and walls have succumbed to the inevitable march of time, as have the people who once lived in these places. Nevertheless, they still provide us with many strong clues as to why they were constructed.

The natural place to start when discussing this question is to look at the obvious 'military' aspect of hillforts. Some archaeologists have suggested that hillforts were used primarily as a means of displaying status, rather than as defended settlements built to deter and repel hostile forces. While there may be some truth in the former argument, the evidence comes down heavily in the favour of the latter and more widely accepted one. Of course not all hillforts would have been military in character and some were probably cattle corrals, tribal meeting places or even religious centres. However, all in all, the architecture and location of many hillforts surely reveals, as James Dyer asserts in *Ancient Britain*, 'that the defence of the interior was all important'. Barry Cunliffe (the main authority on Iron Age Britain) provides further support for the idea that hillforts were defended settlements: '[I]t could be argued that forts were essentially objects of display with no military significance, but while some element of display may well have been involved, there can be little doubt that the siting and construction of the forts was carried out with a firm eye on the defensive potentialities of the situation'.

Aside from the obvious fact that many hillforts were located on hilltops or promontories (why build them here if defence was not a prime concern?), we also have to consider the defences. Why for instance, was it felt necessary to build rampart walkways such as the example observed at Tre'r Ceiri and the ones that must have topped wooden ramparts. Again it seems an unnecessary measure if those inside hillforts were not fearful of attack from enemies and that therefore, patrolling sentries must have used them.

We also have to consider the elaborate entrances built in several hillforts, which as mentioned above must been designed to stop attackers reaching the weakest point of the forts – the gates. There is a chance, that like the formidable ramparts, ditches and walls of hillforts, these entrances were incorporated into some hillforts in order to enhance the prestige of those within. Again though, this seems highly unlikely and the main purpose of elaborate entrances must have been as defensive features.

There is one final architectural feature of hillforts that should be mentioned when considering the defence of hillforts – the *chevaux de frise*. Although these are rare in the British Isles, they can be found guarding some hillforts in Wales (they are commonly found in northern and western parts of Iberia). *Chevaux de frise* consist of small, upright blocks (sometimes pointed) that were set closely together outside the entrances to hillforts and can only have had a defensive function and they would seriously hinder any attacking force. As Michael Senior tells us, the curious name given to these outer defences of pointed stones comes from the term *cheval de frise*, which means 'horse of Friesland'. It appears to have originated during the Dutch war of independence from Spain, when Dutch forces set up sets of spikes in front of weak points in fortifications. One of the finest examples of *chevaux de frise* can be found at the spectacular cliff-top fort of Dun Aengus in Ireland, where it adds to the defensive features of this formidable stone fort.

The most notable example of a *cheavaux de frise* found in Wales comes Pen y Gaer (which looks over the Conwy Valley in north-western Wales), where two areas of pointed stones with an outer ditch guard the approach to its entrance. Interestingly, Hogg states in the excavation report on Garn Boduan and Tre'r Ceiri that the *chevaux de frise* at Pen y Gaer 'can be paralleled exactly in Central Spain'. Evidence such as this and the apparent rarity of *chevaux de frise* at other hillforts in the British Isles perhaps hints at the arrival of small groups of Mediterranean immigrants here during the Iron Age. As mentioned above however, other Welsh examples of cheavaux de frise are known at the hillforts of Craig Gwrtheyrn in Carmarthenshire and at Caer Euni in Pembrokeshire. An early example was also discovered beneath a later rampart at Castell Henllys and as Frances Lynch suggests in *Prehistoric Wales*, this may indicate that *Chevaux de frise* were actually more widespread and earlier in date than has generally been assumed.

It could also be that pointed wooden stakes were also probably quite commonly used in the same way as the *Cheavaux de frise* at hillforts, but finding evidence of them is obviously difficult and is also hampered by a lack of excavation outside hillforts. Nevertheless, an example has been identified at the hillfort of south Barrule on the Isle of Man, which suggests that more may come to light in the future.

It would not just have been people that the hillforts defended, but probably also grain, livestock and other commodities as well. We have already seen the evidence from Croft Ambrey, where the large amount of four-posters suggests that this was an important grain storage centre. Indeed, in *Prehistoric Europe*, Barry Cunliffe feels that the hillforts of southern Britain were built primarily as places concerned with 'the acquisition and storage of food surpluses'.

While many hillforts may have been untouched by conflict, fighting certainly took place at some of these sites and archaeological discoveries at hillforts both in Wales and England provide confirmation of this. At the hillforts of Maiden Bower (Bedfordshire) and Arbury Banks (Herefordshire), the skeletons of adults and children were thrown unceremoniously into the ditches and hint at violent and successful attacks, which overran the hillforts. Even stronger evidence for attacks on hillforts was discovered at Bredon Hill and Sutton Walls in Worcesteshire. At Bredon hill the remains of bodies which appear to have been hacked to pieces were discovered in the passage that led to the gate, while at Sutton Walls, skeletons displaying weapon marks were casually tossed into ditches that surrounded the hillfort.

As mentioned above some of the burials found at hillforts relate to the battles that took place at them during the Roman conquest and those found at Maiden Castle may provide a brutal snapshot of the Roman attack on this magnificent hillfort. During his excavations at the site in the 1930's, the renowned archaeologist, Mortimer Wheeler discovered a mass grave containing 38 bodies belonging to 23 men and 11 women. Ten of the male skeletons had extensive cut marks to the skull, which must have been caused by sword blows and the distinctive hole in one skull showed that a spear had pierced it. The most telling evidence however, was the Roman spearhead (or 'balista' bolt) that was found embedded in the spine of one of the skeletons. Wheeler interpreted this grave as evidence for the attack on Maiden Castle by Vespasian's legionaries during the Roman conquest, with the dead of the vanquished defenders thrown unceremoniously into a mass grave, by Roman soldiers. Although it now seems more likely that friendly hands buried the people in the grave, the evidence does point to a successful Roman assault on Maiden Castle hillfort.

Sling-stone dumps have also been found at several hillforts and reveal at the very least, that people within hillforts were prepared for attacks. In comparison to the incredible killing power of modern armies the use of slingers in Iron Age warfare may seem somewhat laughable. However, we should not underestimate the effectiveness of the sling as a deadly weapon and advancing uphill, while under fire from determined and skilled teams of slingers, cannot have made hillfort assaults easy.

As we saw above, small numbers of sling-stones have been found at Garn Boduan, Castell Odo and Tre'r Ceiri and they are known at other hillforts in Wales. For example, at Moel Hiraddug (Flintshire), a sling-stone dump was found inside a round-house that was situated near to the passage that led to the fort's gates, while at Castell Henllys, a huge sling-stone dump was also found. It is extremely likely that Castell Henllys was assaulted at some point, as the gates and part of the rampart were burnt down. It is also possible that Fridd Faldwyn (Montgomeryshire) was also attacked, as here too, the timber-laced rampart was set on fire and the stones that were also incorporated into the rampart became vitrified or fused together because of the great heat created by the fire. At Crickley Hill, the first Iron Age fort on the site had been burnt down, when the attackers piled brushwood against its ramparts.

Large numbers of vitrified hillforts are found in Scotland and while not all may have been burnt during assaults (i.e.

accidental or even ritual burning could account for some), it is more probable that many were.

The accounts of the classical authors seem to provide further confirmation that many hillforts in the Iron Age were built because this was a dangerous time, when the threat of attack by enemy forces was never far away. Of course, such accounts should be treated warily, as they were being written for a Roman audience and contain a certain amount of bias. Nevertheless, they are still hugely useful sources for providing information on the Celts at war.

In *Histories II*, Polybius is particularly informative in this respect and paints a vivid picture of the Celts in battle, telling us how such battles began with opposing chariots riding up down the massed ranks of the enemy. While doing so, the charioteers screamed at their opponents to scare them and no doubt this early form of psychological warfare consisted of many curses and the general disparagement of the enemy's bravery and worth. Meanwhile, to the rear the opposing forces added to this verbal assault by screaming war-cries and banging on the sides of the wagons that carried them to battle. In the next stage of battle the warriors were driven into the field, where they dismounted to lay down personal challenges to their opponents. After these individual battles were concluded, all the combatants on either side became involved and it is hard to imagine how terrifying and brutal these larger battles must have been.

Of course, Polybius' account relates to battles fought in the open, but Julius Caesar tells us in his *Gallic Wars* that attacks did take place at hillforts and informs us of the methods of warfare that were employed in such attacks. It appears that the attackers threw an array of missiles at the defenders on the ramparts and then with shields above their heads they ran in under this 'covering fire' and set fire to the ramparts. The Romans also used similar tactics in battle and the famous *testudo* (lit.'tortoise'), where the legionaries would interlock their shields to form a protective roof and wall around them was often used to good effect. The ancient historian Tacitus tells us of an example of the *testudo* being used in an attack on a hillfort in the Severn Valley (during a campaign led by Ostorious the Roman Governor), where the deployment of the *testudo* enabled the Romans to advance uphill and destroy the hillfort's walls. Whether the Romans or the Celts were the first to use the *testudo* in battle is open to question, but we do know that the Romans replaced their smaller, round shields with the longer and broader type favoured by the Celts, which were more suited to the *testudo*.

Some scholars have argued that Celtic warfare was in fact largely small-scale and fought between 'champions' on either side. While such 'duels' must have occurred, archaeological evidence such as battle casualties buried in ditches, sling stone dumps and the burning of hillforts indicate that large-scale forces were also involved in Iron Age warfare – as do the impressive fortifications found at many hillforts.

There must have been a number of reasons behind the attacks that took place on hillforts. In some cases, these attacks may have been motivated by personal factors – such as the desire to avenge the murder of a kinsman, but in many cases it was probably the acquisition of wealth that was the greatest driving force behind these attacks. This wealth would have come not only in the form of livestock, grain, and other commodities such as metal goods, but also in the form of people. It is well known that slaves played an important part in the continental Iron Age economy and the slave chains found at Llyn Cerrig Bach, which were mentioned in the previous chapter, provide grim testimony to a similar state of affairs in the British Iron Age. The ancient historian Strabo provides us with literary evidence for the slave trade in Iron Age Britain and tells us that they were one of the main exports to the Roman world, along with corn, cattle, gold, silver, hides and hunting dogs.

## Hillforts and society in the peninsula
While it would be dangerous to assume that all hillforts can be socially interpreted in the same way, it is highly likely, as Barry Cunliffe has suggested that many represent 'the emergence of a warrior leadership with coercive power over, and presumably responsibility for a group of clans'. Whether a similar social structure existed in the peninsula during the Iron Age is hard to say for sure, but it seems probable that the

three major hillforts in the peninsula (i.e. Tre'r Ceiri, Garn Boduan and Garn Fadrun) were high-status sites where powerful leaders and their retinue lived. There is no doubt that a powerful aristocracy sat at the head of later Iron Age society and Boudica 'queen of the Iceni' provides a lasting reminder of this aristocracy. Leaders of such wealth and power may not have existed in the earlier stages of the Iron Age, but it is difficult to accept that society was egalitarian at this time. Indeed, we have already seen hints of an unequal society in the Neolithic and Bronze Age burial monuments of the peninsula and social stratification must have become even more marked during the Iron Age.

Perhaps in the smaller hillforts and other Iron Age settlements of the peninsula lived people of a lesser status who ultimately answered to their 'overlords' who lived above them in the larger hillforts. Such interpretations are of course simplistic and do not prove that warrior chiefs and their associated retainers sat in the large hillforts of the peninsula looking out over their subjects, even if the evidence points to this.

However, there are perhaps stronger indicators that a warrior aristocracy was living in the major hillforts of the peninsula during the Iron Age and Roman period. It will be remembered that a gold-plated torc, fibula and pin were found at Tre'r Ceiri. Although they are likely to date to the Roman period, they would have been worn by people of high status and are surely indicative of an élite. In this respect, as we have also seen, two beads of Egyptian manufacture were also found within the hillfort. Exactly how these exotic items reached this isolated corner of Europe is a mystery but they perhaps suggest long-distance contact and exchange between important people. It finally remains to consider the sword pommel or shield boss found in the likely grave below Tre'r Ceiri; could this be the final resting place of an aristocratic warrior? It would be interesting if the area around the graves was investigated further, and brought may bring other burials to light.

**Evidence for attacks on the peninsula's hillforts**
As with other hillforts in the British Isles, the fortifications

and location of the peninsula's hillforts suggest that at the very least, their inhabitants were prepared for attack. The sling stones that have been found at Tre'r Ceiri, Castell Odo and Garn Boduan also lend further support to this idea – although it has to be admitted that they are few in number. Is there though, any firmer evidence that hillforts in the peninsula suffered at the hands of hostile forces? The answer to this question seems to be 'yes' and as mentioned previously, this evidence is found at Castell Odo and it appears that the settlement here may have been attacked not once, but twice, during its history of occupation.

As seen above, the fist settlement at Castell Odo appears to have consisted of an undefended hilltop settlement, which on the basis of the evidence was probably built at the end of the Bronze Age. The archaeological evidence also strongly suggests that the first phase of occupation at the site ended when Castell Odo was overrun by an attacking force, which set the settlement on fire.

The first piece of evidence for the deliberate burning of the first settlement at Castell Odo comes from the wooden houses that were built during this time. Leslie Alcock tells us that '[t]wo of the posts of 'Timber Building B' were found reduced to charcoal, while the floor of 'Timber Building A' was covered with a layer of ash and fine charcoal which probably represents the burning down of the roof.' Of course, it could be argued that these houses burned down accidentally, but this theory is weakened somewhat by further evidence found at the site.

Alcock also discovered that a wooden stockade had began to be set up around the first settlement. The evidence for the unfinished stockade consisted of a 12 ft section of rock-cut trench, built on the western edge of the settlement, which also contained packing stone stones to help secure the timber posts of the stockade. It should also be noted here, that Alcock suggested that this evidence could possibly represent the remains of the end wall of a rectangular wooden house. However, in regard to this possibility he says, '[i]t is far more likely that we have here evidence for a defensive palisade which, it will appear, was never completed'. It seems likely that this palisade was never completed because it was deliberately burnt down. Proof that it had burnt down was provided by the fact that the packing stones were all heavily burnt and that were also several areas of charcoal, which must have been the remains of burnt posts.

It has to be admitted that this evidence is not conclusive proof of attack at Castell Odo, but it is hard to disagree with Alcock's reading of it: 'In a moment of external danger it had been decided to fortify Mynydd Ystum with a timber stockade... Its defences unfinished, the settlement was readily stormed. Its houses were burnt down and the palisade near Timber Building B was similarly destroyed.'

Such evidence is likely to point to inter-tribal warfare in the peninsula during the Late Bronze Age, but it is also possible that an enemy force from elsewhere attacked the site and we should perhaps bear in mind the proximity of Ireland in this respect? While warfare may not have been endemic in the Late Bronze Age, as in earlier periods, it certainly existed and archaeological evidence from England provides proof of this.

At Tormarton in Gloucestershire, a Late Bronze Age burial containing the skeletons of three young men in their late teens or early twenties was found during the laying of a gas pipeline. A lozenge-shaped hole was found in the pelvis of one of the skeletons and it is clear that this had been made by a socketed spearhead. Evidence from one of the other skeletons provided even more graphic evidence of the deadly violence that could strike communities of the Late Bronze Age. Part of a spearhead was found wedged in the spine (which would have caused instant paralysis) and further holes in the pelvis and damage to the skull, probably show how this young man was brutally finished off as he lay in agony on the ground.

Further skeletal evidence for Late Bronze Age warfare was found at Dorchester-on-Thames (Oxfordshire) and consisted of a spearhead embedded in the pelvis of a male skeleton. It seems that it had snapped off as the spear was being violently withdrawn from the victim's body.

After the destruction of the first settlement at Castell Odo people probably stopped living there for short while, as indicated by a thin layer of soil that had been washed downhill to cover the remains of the stockade and Timber Building B. However people soon returned to live at the site, which continued to be occupied into the Iron Age and Romano-British period. Whether the people who reoccupied the site after its short abandonment were the ones who attacked and burnt down the first settlement is hard to say, but it does seem quite likely.

In the third stage of the settlement's history, ramparts revetted with stone walls (Alcock estimates these were around 10-12 ft wide and some 4-5ft high) enclosed a settlement that contained circular houses with stone walls. The settlement was approached by a 'cobbled road' that led to the entrance that was closed by a large wooden gate.

Leslie Alcock tells us that the next and last significant stage of Castell Odo's history *(Phase 4)* 'was initiated by a drastic reduction of the banks of Castell Odo, in which they were deprived of whatever military value they had ever possessed'. It appears that the revetment walls on either side of the gate were demolished and the large stones removed, which, as Alcock says, 'must have left the entrance as an open breach through the banks'. The revetments to the rear of the two ramparts were also slighted and in some cases demolished completely and thus, stone roundhouses were subsequently built over the ruined ramparts.

Whether the above evidence indicates that Castell Odo was actually attacked again, during a later phase of occupation is without doubt, open to question, but it does strongly suggest that the site was deliberately slighted so that its military effectiveness was much reduced. However, who was responsible for this apparently act of deliberate destruction, is far from clear.

Alcock suggests that the Romans were responsible for the conversion of Castell Odo from a hillfort to an open settlement and he feels that 'Llŷn was forcibly demilitarized by the Romans, who then left it as unadministered tribal territory, largely outside the range of Roman influences'. However, his theory rests solely on the finding of an intact saddle quern used as building material in the floor of Hut 8/11 which was associated with the last phase of occupation at the site. He can find no other reason for the use of a perfectly good saddle quern as flooring material, other than it 'had been rendered obsolete by the speedier rotary quern'. As the latter querns are likely to have been introduced into Wales during the Roman occupation, Alcock therefore sees this as evidence that Castell Odo was 'demilitarized' by the Romans around this time.

It has to be admitted that Alcock's theory rests on rather tenuous evidence and there is precious little else to suggest that the Romans were ever actually at Castell Odo, but nevertheless, this theory should not be totally discounted. It could be that the slighting of Castell Odo was related to a Roman campaign in northern Wales, probably during the autumn of 77AD, which was sparked by the massacre of a Roman cavalry unit by warriors of the tribe known as the Ordovices. Although the Ordovices lived in the Snowdonia region, the Romans may also have decided to send a force further west into the peninsula. However, while this remains a possibility, as Michael Senior has pointed out, the evidence that other hillforts in the peninsula were 'demilitarized' by the Romans is lacking and it therefore seems odd that the Romans singled out Castell Odo.

Therefore, the above evidence at Castell Odo could again be related to inter-tribal hostilities breaking out between kin groups or clans of the Gangani tribe, who lived in the peninsula and along the northern coast of Welsh as far as Conwy (a tribe of the same name also lived in north-west Ireland and therefore the two tribes were presumably related). It is also possible that as with the likely attack on the Late Bronze Age settlement at Castell Odo, those responsible for the later slighting of the defences at the site, came from outside Wales.

We will probably never know who was responsible for the slighting of Castell Odo's defences, but it is possible that the Romans left the natives of the peninsula in isolation, feeling they offered no serious threat to the empire. Therefore they may have been content to keep watch on them from the major fortress at Segontium in nearby Caernarfon and the fort situated at Llystyn, near Bryncir on the eastern edge of the peninsula. Interestingly, pottery found at this site (which has now probably been obliterated), indicates a Roman presence at the fort from c. 80-100 AD, which ties in with the date of the Roman campaign in Wales, mentioned above.

It is clear from the evidence that not only were the major hillforts intensively occupied in the Roman period, but that they were also strongly defended. As seen above, the evidence indicates that the defences of the major hillforts were further enlarged and strengthened in a later phase of occupation. It is quite possible that these later architectural developments reveal the native response to the Roman threat and date to the early conquest period.

The major hillforts of the peninsula would therefore have been very formidable places in the Roman period and it is possible therefore, that their 'impregnability' played some part in the apparent Roman decision to leave the peninsula as an unadministered tribal territory. Michael Senior has said that the Romans would not be keen to attack Tre'r Ceiri 'because not even under the *testudo* would the legionaries dare to struggle up such a hill, with a barrage of stones raining down on them'. Any reader who has visited the magnificent hillfort of Tre'r Ceiri, will see why Michael Senior has made the above suggestion and Garn Boduan and Garn Fadrun can probably be viewed in the same light.

## Chapter 10

# Early Christian Stones and Holy Wells

### The Arrival of Christianity

We cannot say for sure when Christianity first arrived in Wales, but both literary and archaeological evidence indicates that it was present well before Constantine III withdrew the last legions from Britain around 407 AD. It seems safe to assume that there were Christians among the legionary forces that were stationed in Britain during the Roman occupation, though they would have been few in number. Also, the Christian writer Tertullian (c. 160-240 AD) tells us that although not widespread, Christianity was practiced in certain parts of Britain. We also know that British bishops from London, York and Lincoln attended the first Church council at Arles in 314 AD. Also worth mentioning are the three British, Christian martyrs – Alban, Aaron and Julius, who were probably put to death by the Romans in the middle of the third century.

The archaeological evidence for Christianity in Roman Britain is slight, but it provides confirmation that although their numbers must have been small, Christians were living in Romano-British towns and cities. The earliest archaeological evidence that we have appears to come from the Romano-British city of Corinium (Cirencester) and consists of a fragment of red wall-plaster found in a house at the site, which has a cross composed of the words *Pater Noster* scratched on its surface. As Nora Chadwick has said of this meagre but significant find, '[I]ts appearance seems to attest the presence of Christians in the Romano-British city of Corinium in the third, or even in the second century'. However, it is not until the fourth century that more concrete evidence of Christianity in Roman Britain begins to emerge. Perhaps the finest evidence we have for comes from the villa discovered at Hinton Saint Mary in Dorset in 1963, where the central motif of an exquisite mosaic was an image of Christ with the Christian 'Chi-Ro' symbol behind his head. It seems that this was originally, a pagan symbol used by the Greeks, but the early Christians adopted and adapted it in the third century AD. A mosaic floor depicting similar Christian iconography has also been found at a Roman villa at Frampton in Dorset.

A number of likely fourth century, Romano-British Churches have also been found and examples include those found at Butt Road in Colchester and Icklingham in Suffolk. At the latter of these sites, two circular lead tanks bearing the Chi-Ro monogram were found and it is probable that they were used in baptisms. Mention should also be made of the late Roman cemetery at Poundbury in Dorchester. Here, around a thousand graves have been discovered, with many of them oriented east-west in the Christian manner. Many of the deceased were buried without grave goods though in one grave, a pierced coin bearing the Chi-Ro symbol was found.

Scholars such as E.G. Bowen have argued that Christianity died out after the Romans withdrew from Britain and was then reintroduced from abroad during the fifth century. While there is some truth in his argument, considering the discoveries above, it seems hard to believe that Christianity simply 'left' with the Romans and more likely that it survived sporadically and was still practised by a minority. There is in fact some evidence from south-eastern Wales that points towards this state of affairs as being the most likely. This evidence consists of the discovery of Christian graves (orientated east-west) cutting through the mosaic floor of a fourth century villa at Llanilltud Fawr and a possible early church built just above the ruins of a Roman bath-house at Caer-went.

It would be safe to say that by the end of the fifth century Christianity had a firm foothold in the British Isles and the earliest Christian stones and holy wells of Wales date to this time. Fortunately, we have several fine examples of both in our area of interest and we will turn our attention to the former monuments first. The Early Christian stones and holy wells of the peninsula are of great significance because, as is the case elsewhere in Wales, they bear witness to the founding of the Celtic Church and the conversion of its people to the new religion that was to have such a huge impact world-wide.

## EARLY CHRISTIAN MEMORIAL STONES

Following the criteria set out in V.E. Nash-Williams' magisterial study – *The Early Christian Monuments of Wales* – the Early Christian stones of the peninsula can be placed into two groups. The first group consists of *Simple Inscribed Stones* dating from the fifth to the seventh century AD, while the second features Cross-decorated stones dating from the seventh to ninth century.

## SIMPLE INSCRIBED STONES

As the inscriptions on these stones show, they were erected as gravestones or memorials to the deceased and in some cases, burials have been found in association with them. In fact, as we shall see below we have an example of this from the peninsula. As Leslie Alcock has said, they are 'memorials of the upper classes, both lay and ecclesiastical'. It should perhaps also be remembered that some of these people were still largely pagan in their outlook and by setting up such memorial stones they were simply paying 'lip service' to the new religion of Christianity. In this respect, Sam Turner has suggested that the Early Christian stones of Wales 'may have more to do with showing personal power than with conversion to Christianity' and that they 'clearly do emphasise elite power over settled land'. It is a theory that is certainly worth bearing in mind, particularly when considering the earliest 'Christian' memorial stones.

As is the case elsewhere in Wales, the inscriptions were carved on monoliths of varying shape and size. It is also evident that former standing stones of the Bronze Age were sometimes used for inscriptions and thus these former pagan monuments became 'christianised'. Simple Inscribed Stones are also found in Devon, Cornwall, Somerset, the Isle of Man and also in Northumbria and Scotland.

On these monuments the inscriptions commemorating the dead are written in Latin or in the intriguing Ogam script and a number of Christian stones also feature bilingual inscriptions. As Nash-Williams tells us the Ogam alphabet consisted of 'twenty letters, together with supplementary symbols, arranged in sets *(aicme)* of five, represented by groups of notches of strokes, numbering from one to five, variously disposed along a central guide-line'. The sharp edge of the stone being inscribed would normally be used as the guide-line and on the Welsh Christian stones the inscriptions usually read upwards.

Peter Berresford Ellis says that Ogam developed in Ireland at the start of the Christian period and was named after the Celtic god *Ogma* (*Ogmios* to the British and Continental Celts), who was the god of eloquence and literacy. Nash-Williams agrees with Berresford Ellis and states that Ogam was 'a system of writing, based probably on a manual alphabet, invented in Ireland before the fifth century A.D'. However, *The Penguin Dictionary of Archaeology* says of Ogam, '[I]t is believed to have originated in Ireland or South Wales as a secret script around c. 3 AD'. Therefore there seems to be some uncertainty as to where Ogam originated, though the fact that the greatest concentration of Ogam inscriptions is found in south-west Munster, perhaps points to an Irish birthplace for the Ogam alphabet.

The idea that Ogam was invented as a secret script is an attractive theory and it may well be that members of the Druidical class used it as a way of recording important aspects of their lore and teachings that they wished to keep hidden. As Berresford Ellis also notes, '[f]rom later Irish texts written in Latin script we hear that in earlier times Ogam was used to write ancient stories and sagas; it was incised on bark or wands of hazel and aspen'. Unfortunately, though not surprisingly, it is only the Ogam inscriptions written on the Christian stones that have survived, though perhaps one day a remarkable discovery will be made of an Ogam inscription written on wood. Although Christian stones featuring Ogam inscriptions are rare in northern Wales, one still survives in the peninsula.

When it comes to the origins of the Latin inscriptions on

the Early Christian stones we are perhaps on firmer ground. As Nash-Williams points out, these inscriptions 'both in language and lettering, are akin to the Early Christian inscriptions of the western Roman Empire, especially Gaul, and thus indicate direct and continuing intercourse between Wales and Gaul in the sub-Roman period'. It is hard to disagree with Nash-Williams when he says '[i]t is tempting to see in this intercourse evidence of a deliberate and sustained evangelizing effort on the part of the Great Gaulish monasteries directed towards the conversion of Wales and the neighbouring Celtic regions'. Nora Chadwick follows a similar line of reasoning and says '[t]he real inspiration of the Celtic churches...in Both Britain and Ireland, was the missionary effort inspired by the monastic ideals of fifth-century Gaul'.

## CROSS-DECORATED STONES

More equivocally Christian than the inscribed stones are the monoliths featuring incised and carved crosses. These are later than the former monuments and mainly date from the seventh to ninth centuries when Christianity would have been firmly entrenched amongst the early Medieval communities of Wales (though pre-Christian beliefs must still have played a significant part in people's lives). Cross-decorated stones appear to be largely confined to mid and southern Wales though the peninsula also boasts a small but significant concentration of these monuments. The crosses that appear on the cross-decorated stones of the peninsula consist of the simple, *linear* type, which originated amongst the ancient Greeks and Romans, and *ring-crosses* which are derived from the Chi-Ro symbol.

# SIMPLE INSCRIBED AND CROSS-DECORATED CHRISTIAN STONES IN THE PENINSULA

## SIMPLE INSCRIBED CHRISTIAN STONES

### Plas Glyn y Weddw *(100, 101)*

These are among the most interesting of the Early Christian stones of the peninsula, as they were discovered in association with a grave, which was found about 50 yards from the larger of the two standing stones found at Tir Gwyn. The stones appear to have been found in the early nineteenth century and first recorded in *Lewis's Topographical Dictionary of Wales* (1833). Lewis says: 'In a field called Maen Hir [the Welsh word for a standing stone] ...a very curious grave was recently discovered, containing some remains of human bones; the body appeared to have been deposited on the gravel with the feet towards the north and on each side was a slab of chert-stone, six feet long, curiously wrought. On these stones, forming the eastern and western sides of the grave, are inscriptions in rude Roman characters, and above them was a flat stone covered with soil'. A more detailed account of the grave and the stones, written by Sir T.D. Love Jones-Parry, appeared in *Archaeologia Cambrenis* in 1847. He tells us that as well as the hexagonal shaped side-stones, there was a head stone and a foot stone and that the grave contained the bones of a large man (he is said to have been about 7 ft tall!). At some point after their discovery, the stones were removed to the Ashmolean Museum in Oxford, but they have since been returned to their rightful home and now stand in the entrance to the fine country house at Plas Glyn y Weddw in Llanbedrog. Both stones are made of local basalt, measure around 5.5 ft in height and probably date to the sixth century.

Although it is now somewhat difficult to make out the inscriptions on the stones, both feature Latin and the slightly taller of the stones features two lines reading vertically downwards:

*IOVENALI FILI / ETERNI / HIC IACIT*
*(Iovenalis son of Eternus. He lies here)*

On the other stone a single name is inscribed:
*VENDESETLI (Vendesetl)*

Nash-Williams tells us that '[t]he form *Vendesetl* preserves the name of the 6th-century saint Gwynhoedl, patron of the ancient church of Llangwynadl'. The church of St Gwynhoedl at Llangwynadl, which presumably stands on or very near the site of the earliest church, lies about 10 miles from the burial site on the western coast of Llŷn. There is a reference to Gwynhoedl in a thirteenth century Welsh manuscript of the early saints, which reads: 'Gwynodl or Gwynoedyl, son of King Seithennin, from Maes Gyddno, whose land was inundated by the sea. Llangwnodl in Lleyn.' The children of King Seithennin are said to have been saints at the early church founded at Bangor.

In regard to the other inscription not much can be said other than that 'Iovenalis' is a form of the Roman name *Juvenal* and it is possible that the village of Edern in Llŷn is named after *Eternus* his father. It seems also that *Tir Gwyn* is so named because of its association with the burial, though as J. Rhys says in *Archaeologia Cambrenis* (1877), 'it would be difficult perhaps to determine whether Tir Gwyn...meant the white or sacred land, or the land of Gwyn, that is of Gwynhoedl'.

There is also the mystery of who was actually buried in the grave. The fact that two separate, inscribed memorial stones were used in the grave, presumably indicates that they formerly stood above ground somewhere else, but were taken down at some point and reused as side-stones in the grave? An account of the stones in Archaeologia Cambrensis (1925) deepens the mystery further, as the local landowner reported that other stone slabs similar to the one found covering the burial had been found when the field was being ploughed. This indicates that there may have been an Early Christian cemetery in this area and it would certainly be interesting to see what would turn up here, if the site was reinvestigated by archaeologists.

Finally, although it is a possibility, as mentioned in Chapter 5, it is unlikely that the two standing stones were contemporary with the burial and are likely to be of prehistoric origin. It is more probable that a refusal to completely discard older, pagan beliefs or a desire to christianise a pagan site drew people to this site in the Early Christian period.

### Saint Hywyn's (102)

The two inscribed Christian stones that now stand in a corner of the ancient and tranquil church (c. 1100 BC) of St Hywyn's at Aberdaron, display the finest inscriptions seen on the inscribed Christian stones of the peninsula. They also provide us with a fascinating record of important figures who belonged to an Early Christian, religious community in the peninsula. The stones date from the late fifth or early sixth century and stand around 3 ft in height. The inscriptions on them read:

*SENACUS / PRSB (presbyter) / HIC IACIT / CVM MULTITV /*
*DNEM / FRATRVM / PRESBYTER*
*(added to the bottom of the stone at a later date)*

*(Senacus the Priest lies here with the multitude of the brethren)*

*VERACIUS / PBR / HIC / IACIT*
*(Veracius the Priest lies here)*

As Alcock has said of the reference to the *multitude of brethren* on the Senacus stone: '[t]he phrase implies burial in the cemetery of a monastery' and this idea is definitely worth considering. The stones were found under the slopes of Mynydd Anelog and it is known that a fifth century hermitage once existed in this area. It is possible therefore, that Senacus and Veracius were important members of this hermitage which would have been used as a place of retreat by the monks of the early Celtic church. The possible foundation trench of a later medieval church (Capel Verach) can still be seen under Mynydd Anelog and although no traces of the earlier hermitage survive, once again this would be an area worthy of archaeological investigation. It may be that traces of the hermitage still exist below the surface and perhaps it is even possible that some of the brethren of Senacus still lie in their graves at this ancient site?

### Llangian *(103)*

This stone stands in the graveyard of the picturesque church in the village of Llangian which lies about two miles outside the popular holiday resort of Abersoch. The rectangular stone, which has a flat area cut away for a sun-dial, stands about 3.5 ft in height and features one of the most fascinating inscriptions found on the inscribed Early Christian stones of the peninsula. This says:

*MELI MEDICI / FILI MARTINI / IACIT (Melus the Doctor, son of Martinus. He lies here)*

Nash-Williams has pointed out that it is highly unusual to see the secular profession of the deceased mentioned on Early Christian stones and this seems to be the only example in Britain, where a medicus (doctor), is commemorated. This stone therefore provides us with a unique insight into early Christian society in the peninsula and indicates that it was functioning on quite a sophisticated level.

### Llanaelhaearn *(105, 106)*

The church at Llanaelhaearn not only boasts two inscribed Christian stones but also what is probably a former cross-decorated stone and an unmarked stone slab, which may also date to the early Christian period. The first inscribed stone (fifth early sixth century) stands near the entrance to the church in the graveyard and measures about 3 ft in height. As with one of the memorial stones found at Tir Gwyn, the stone is inscribed with a single name reading downwards:

*MELI _ TVu (Melitus)*

The other inscribed stone (of the same date as the above) is built into the wall inside the church and appears to provide us with a fascinating and unique example of a tombstone commemorating the death of an immigrant who settled and died in the peninsula. There are two lines of inscription on the stone:

*ALIORTVS / ELMETIACO / HIC IACET (Aliortus the Elmetian lies here)*

It is known that Elmet (Elfed) was the name of an ancient British Kingdom, which roughly corresponds to what is now the West Riding of Yorkshire and as Nash-Williams has noted, the stone provides us with a '[s]light but valuable insight into contemporary political and tribal divisions' in northern Britain. Why Aliortus came to the peninsula will never be known, but it is evident that he ended his days here.

## Llannor *(107)*

This stone (dating to the sixth century) measures around 5 ft in height and stands inside the porch of Llannor church. The inscription consists of three lines:

FIGVLINI FILI / LOCVLITI / HIC IACIT *(Figulinus, son of Loculitus. He lies here)*

As with Melitus at Llanaelhaearn and Icorix below, nothing more is known about Figulinus and Loculitus.

## Bryncir

This appears to be the only definite example from the peninsula, of an Early Christian inscribed stone that displays an Ogam inscription as well as a Latin one. A possible Ogam stone also exists near Mynydd Carnguwch, but it is hard to say whether the 'inscription' is man-made or simply natural markings on the stone. The Bryncir Ogam stone was found at Llystyngwyn Farm, on the eastern edge of the peninsula, close to the western boundary of Snowdonia National Park. The stone stands around 3.5 ft in height and dates to the sixth century. The Latin inscription, which is in three lines, reads:

ICORI / FILIVS / POTENT / INI *(Icorix, son of Potentinus)*

The Ogam inscription is inscribed along the top right edge of the stone and reads:

ICORIGAS *(Icorix)*

## CROSS-DECORATED CHRISTIAN STONES

### Llanaelhaearn

There is some uncertainty surrounding this monument, as

the cross carved in the stone can no longer be seen. It seems probable however, that this is the original Christian stone as recorded by Nash-Williams and others and that the cross is no longer visible because of weathering and the lichen that now covers it.

The stone is incorporated into the wall near the south side of the church and measures about 3.5 ft in height. The original cross, which dates from the 7th-9th century, was of the linear type and had wide, slightly splayed arms. As mentioned previously, another unmarked and irregular, stone slab can be seen in the churchyard and its appearance suggests that it is of considerable antiquity. It is perhaps possible that this stone was also an Early Christian memorial stone and once featured a cross or an inscription. However, I have found no record of this and so for the present, it remains a mystery.

### Cefn-Coch

This monument can be found not far from Ffynnon Gybi holy well, but unfortunately time has rendered the cross on the stone rather indistinct. Nevertheless, it can still be just about seen and it is evident that it is an irregular, simple linear cross, with the shaft longer than the arms. Nash-Williams did not record this monument, but Ralegh Radford and Hemp have suggested that it dates to the 6th century.

### Llangybi *(108)*

This cross-decorated stone stands in the church at Llangybi and lies just inside the gate into the churchyard. The stone bears a cross, which has clubbed or 'trilobate' ends on all of its four arms. Nash-Williams gives a general date of the seventh to ninth century for the monument, while Ralegh Radford and Hemp suggest that it dates to the first half of the 7th century.

### Capel Uchaf *(109)*

Unlike the above, this stone features a ring-cross. The stone is located in Upper Clynnog and once stood upright in a wall by the side of the road, but it has since been reset horizontally in a new wall built during alterations to the road. The stone measures about 3.5 ft in height and features a simple ring-cross, which may be as early in date as the 6th century.

## Pistyll

Another example of a ring-cross, is the one carved on a small stone measuring c. 1.5 ft high, which is presently incorporated in a roadside wall about half a mile west of Pistyll Church. The horizontal shaft of the cross extends outside the ring and the ends of each shaft feature 'bifid' ends. Ralegh Radford and Hemp have postulated an 8th-9th century date for the monument.

## Clynnog Fawr *(110)*

Although it is later in date than the above Christian stones, it is worth mentioning the ancient sundial (11th or early 12th century) that still stands in the graveyard of the church of Beuno at Clynnog Fawr. The sundial is situated on top of a tall, narrow slab and consists of an inscribed semicircle that is divided into three radial lines, which end in short cross-bars within circles. Nash-Williams says of the sundial '[t]he divisions follow the octaval system of time-measurement used in Anglo-Saxon England and Ireland, with the 24 hours divided into eight equal periods or 'tides'. The pointers mark the middle of the tides. According to Nash-Williams, no other such sundials are known in Wales and the one at Clynnog Fawr resembles similar examples found in Ireland.

*(For a full inventory of the Early Christian stones of the peninsula see references for Nash-Williams and Ralegh Radford and Hemp in the bibliography)*

## HOLY WELLS IN THE PENINSULA

### Origins of the Holy Wells

That the ancient Celts venerated water is beyond doubt and abundant archaeological evidence strongly suggests similar beliefs in earlier prehistoric periods. In fact, we do have some possible evidence from the peninsula which suggests perhaps, that some of its holy wells were places that were revered by its Neolithic and Bronze Age communities. In many parts of the British Isles, Neolithic tombs (and other prehistoric monuments such as standing stones) lie close to holy wells and there seems to be some association between the two. In Wales, there are numerous examples of this 'well-megalith association' (as Francis Jones calls it) and in the peninsula the megalithic tombs at Bach Wen and Bronheulog and the standing stones at Llyn Glasfryn are located close to the holy wells of Ffynnon Beuno, Ffynon Aelrhiw and Ffynnon Grasi respectively.

Of course, it could be argued that these prehistoric monuments were located near to the wells because the people who raised them had settled near convenient sources of water but the possibility remains that these wells had a religious significance in prehistoric times. However, unless some remarkable evidence turns up, definitively identifying the wells that were venerated by prehistoric communities of the peninsula is practically impossible. Nevertheless, as Francis Jones says in *Holy Wells in Wales* (the standard work on the subject), '[t]here are in Wales wells which must have been sacred even in pre-Christian times, wells transformed from pagan to Christian usages, and wells that claim a purely Christian origin'. It seems very likely that the same can be said of the peninsula's holy wells and that the origins of some of them lie at least as far back as the Iron Age and probably even further.

At the Roman fort of Brocolita (now known as Carrawburgh) in the wild but beautiful landscape of Northumberland we have a rare example of a definite pre-Christian holy well. This site has provided not only evidence of the Celtic veneration of a sacred well, but also fascinating evidence of how the Romans adopted native gods and goddesses in the countries they conquered and incorporated them into their own pantheon of deities. During excavations at the fort a huge number of artefacts were recovered from the well and along with over fourteen thousand coins, twenty-four altars, pottery, glass, bronze figures and a human skull were found in the well. The altars had originally stood near the well and would have been used in religious ceremonies and rituals that took place here and they may have been thrown into the well when Pictish tribes probably attacked the fort in the fourth century. As Brian Bates notes, in his fascinating *The Real Middle Earth*, '[a]rtefacts recovered at the well show that it was dedicated to Coventina, almost certainly a local Celtic goddess who was adopted by the Romans'.

## The 'Christianisation' of the Holy Wells

Early on in the Christian period, those concerned with establishing this new religion in the British Isles realised that if they were to be successful in their aims, some of their efforts would have to be directed against the pagan worship of wells. As Bates has said, '[t]hey wanted instead to invest the powers of water in the Christian god, and in their own intervention as His earthly representatives'. At the Synod of Arles in 452 and later at the Council of Tours in 567, the church denounced the pagan worship of wells, and stated that 'every priest industriously advance Christianity and extinguish heathenism, and forbid the worship of fountains'.

However, although similar condemnations continued to be made by the religious authorities throughout the first millennium, those who were actually charged with spreading the word of god among the Dark Age communities of the British Isles realised that it would be no easy task to turn people away from pagan well worship. Therefore, as Bates further tells us '[t]he Christians did not deny the power of the well. Rather, they appropriated the connection with that power, and the wells were systematically changed in name to associate each of them with an Anglo-Saxon or Celtic saint'. Likewise, the Rev. Elias Owen writes in *Archaeologia Cambrensis* (1890): '[I]t would seem that the early British missionaries perceiving the people's attachment to ancient forms, consecrated or selected particular wells, already in high esteem, for the purposes of holy baptism'.

As will seen below, a number of the holy wells of the peninsula are named after early Celtic missionaries or 'saints' as they are more commonly known and mentioned above, it is probable that at least some of these were converted from pagan to Christian sites. We should be aware though, that such 'conversions' were in reality, simply putting a Christian gloss on former pagan sites and rituals and beliefs that must have harked back to the pre-Christian era, continued to take place at the holy wells. For example, on May Day (which was adopted from the ancient Celtic summer festival of *Beltane*) at Priest's Well near Narberth in Pembrokeshire, the well was dressed with branches of mountain-ash, (a sacred tree of the ancient Celts) and cowslips, while bonfires were lit close to St John's well in Glamorgan. It is known that many fires were lit during the Celtic festival of Beltane, when the 'rebirth' of the land was celebrated.

Of course, one of the most popular beliefs regarding the holy wells was that some of them had healing powers and it is evident that many of the holy wells of Wales were regarded in this way (and some perhaps still are). People visited these wells hoping for a cure for illnesses which ranged from minor ailments such as sore eyes, warts and indigestion to far more serious ailments such as cancer, epilepsy and mental illness. In some cases, sick animals were also brought to holy wells to be cured. In general, people either bathed in the holy well or a from them and water was also taken from them to the bedsides of the sick and even to those of the dying.

It is clear that some of the wells did actually have healing properties because of the chemicals present in the water and such wells would also have been present in the prehistoric and pre-Christian era. This may have given rise to a belief that all wells were sacred and possessed the power to heal, or simply reinforced the idea that water was connected to the otherworld and was the realm of deities and spirits. We perhaps have echoes of these beliefs preserved in the Welsh folk tales (and those from other countries), which often associate wells with fairies. For example, fairies were said to haunt the wells at Llwyn y Ffynnon (Glamorgan), while at a well in Llanreithan (Pembrokeshire), fairies were said to live beneath the well. Jones has made the interesting suggestion that fairies 'may represent the lesser deities rejected by Christianity'.

Clear evidence of the ancient belief in the healing powers of water, has been found at the headwaters of the Seine in France. Archaeological excavations in 1964 discovered a Romano-Celtic sanctuary where over two hundred wooden carvings had been deposited in the water. Many complete human figures were found but also carvings of things such as limbs and eyes and it is obvious that the people who deposited the carvings were asking the goddess Sequana (the Celtic goddess after whom the river is named) to cure their various illnesses and afflictions.

Further confirmation of this is provided by evidence found at another Romano-Celtic healing sanctuary, also found in France at the *Source du Rocher*. Again carved, wooden figures and human body parts were found, as well as a fascinating lead plate which carried a poignant inscription. On it, a group of elderly men had written a plea to the youthful Celtic god of hunting, *Maponos*, imploring him to cure the various ailments of old age – ailments such as rheumatism and failing eyesight.

It is also apparent that people believed that some holy wells had the power to cause harm and they were used as 'cursing-wells', where people would carry out rituals that they hoped would cause harm or misfortune to their enemies. Perhaps the best known of the Welsh cursing-wells was the infamous Ffynnon Elian, at Llandrillo yn Rhos, not far from Conwy. Here, as the Rev. Owen tells us, ' [t]he manner of proceeding in order to curse any one was to go to the well and drop into it a pebble with the initials of the doomed party written thereon'. It was not just pebbles that were used to curse people at Ffynnon Elian, as an inscribed piece of slate featuring the initials RF, OAM, MEM, AGM and M was found in the well (clearly, whoever dropped the slate in the well had several enemies!). Wax 'voodoo' dolls with pins stuck into them were also placed in the well (the above slate had one attached to it) and mention has to be made of a gruesome and bizarre practice that is said to have taken place at the well. This consisted of impaling a frog on a skewer, which would then have two corks stuck on its ends. The frog would then be floated in the well and as Jones records, 'so long as the unfortunate frog remained alive so long would the enemy suffer ill-fortune'.

It is evident that this practice of placing written curses in sacred waters has a long heritage that stretches back into the Romano-Celtic period. For example, at the famous Roman spa at Bath, Romano-Britons deposited thousands of votive objects in the hot springs, among which were curses written on lead or pewter sheets. One implores Minerva, the goddess of the springs, to return a stolen cloak and to punish the perpetrator of this crime and provides us with a fascinating snapshot of daily life at this time.

Another 'modern' ritual at holy wells, which also seems to have had its roots in prehistory, was the practice of making offerings in them and a clear link to the prehistoric past appears to be evident with the offerings of quartz stones made at some holy wells in Wales. Quartz stones have been found at several prehistoric sites in the British Isles and it is evident that they were viewed as being special in some way by the people of this time. Perhaps one of the best examples of this comes from the recumbent stone circles of Aberdeenshire, which as mentioned in Chapter 5 seem to have had some connection with the midsummer full moon. Interestingly, pieces of white quartz have been found scattered within many of these circles and Aubrey Burl has suggested that for the people who erected them, the moon may have been the home of the dead and that the pieces of quartz 'epitomized the distant land of death'.

Pins were also offered at some holy wells and it is known that this strange custom dates back at least as far as the Roman period, when people must have made offerings to the supernatural forces that were associated with them. In fact pins were offered at many of the peninsula's holy wells, and a notable example is Ffynnon Bedrog near Llanbedrog. Here in 1908, a curious, circular container made from black stone was found at the bottom of the well and when opened it was found to be full of pins. It seems probable that many of the pin offerings made at the wells in more recent times, followed a similar line of reasoning and had more to do with pagan rather than Christian beliefs. We know for instance, that at a well near Selby in Yorkshire, young women would drop pins into the well so that the elves that lived there had 'elf-shot' for their bows. In exchange for the pins, the elves would provide the young women with visions of their 'true loves'. Again, as with the Welsh 'fairy-wells' mentioned above, such folk tales may provide lingering traces of the beliefs of people who lived in the ancient, pre-Christian past.

## EXAMPLES OF HOLY WELLS IN THE PENINSULA

**Ffynnon Gybi** *(111, 112, 113, 114)*
This well lies close to the village of Llangybi and is undoubtedly the finest holy well in the peninsula. It also has the added attraction of being situated in one of the most beautiful parts of the peninsula and is therefore well worth visiting.

The well is dedicated to the early Celtic saint, Cybi, who is said to have crossed over from Ireland in the 6th century and founded the first church at Llangybi. The remains that can be seen today represent a pair of well chambers (the smaller chamber lies just behind the larger one) and a caretaker's cottage and a stone 'privy' can also be seen close to the wells.

The cottage and latrine were built in the mid 17th century by William Price, and although it is not certain at what date the well chambers were built, the wells themselves probably date back thousands of years. The masonry of the largest well chamber does look ancient and it could possibly date back to the Early Christian period. However, the Royal Commission feels the appearance of this chamber is probably 'due to conscious archaism on the part of the 18th-century squire'.

As with the other wells of the peninsula, people would come to Ffynnon Gybi to bathe and drink its waters and it is said to have been particularly good for treating eye disorders. In fact it has been said that a Sion Rhydderch, who had been blind for around thirty years, regained his sight after he bathed his eyes for three weeks with water from the well.

## Ffynnon Aelrhiw *(115, 116)*

Unfortunately, this well is now in a ruinous state and largely covered by undergrowth. Nevertheless, traces of paving and the wall that surrounded the well still survive and these are thought to be 17th century in date. Originally, stone seats were built around the well, but it is now hard to discern any evidence of these. It is said that the water from the well cured skin disorders and that it was particularly good at curing a skin disease known as *'Man Aeliw'* (the mark or spot of Aeliw). Although, not now much remains of the well and it is a shame that it has been allowed to fall into negelct, there are fine views from here across Porth Neigwl and in the summertime it is a very tranquil spot.

## Ffynnon Saint *(117)*

Perhaps the most secluded of the peninsula's holy wells, this monument is located in a peaceful grove above the forestry plantation on the lower, north-eastern slopes of Mynydd Rhiw. The well is surrounded by thick boulder walls and has two sets of steps that lead down into it and although the walls and steps certainly look old it is not clear when they were added to the well. Ffynon Saint is said to have cured eye ailments and women visited it on Dydd Iau Dyrchafael (Ascension Thursday) to wash their eyes and offer pins to the well.

## Ffynnon Beuno *(118, 119)*

This attractive and well cared for monument, is one of the finest holy wells in the peninsula. The stone basin that contains the well is surrounded by seating on three sides and a stone wall, which measures about 2m in height surrounds it; a set of steps lead into the well. It is said that in earlier times, people took scrapings from stone columns within the nearby church of Beuno at Clynnog Fawr and mixed it with a bottle of well water to make a healing potion. The 16th century antiquarian, John Leyland is said to have mentioned that heifers were offered to the well and although what form this 'offering' took is unclear, it seems unlikely that it was sacrificial in nature. The architectural details that can be seen today are thought to be medieval in date, with later additions.

## Ffynnon Fyw

This impressive and well-preserved well is situated on the outskirts of Mynytho, not far from Foel Gron. The well consists of a stone-walled enclosue that measures some 7.5m by 2.5m. There are two well chambers and people visiting the well would bathe in the larger well and drink from the smaller one.Steps at one end of the well give access to the wells. The waters of Ffynnon Fyw are said to have cured blindness and the well was dedicated to saint Curig, who founded a chaple nearby. Ffynnon Fyw is obviously well cared for by the locals and is surrounded by a wooden fence. There also seems to have been some modern restoration work to the stone walls surrounding the two wells.

## Ffynnon Aelhaearn *(120)*

Unfortunately, this holy well was enclosed by brick walls and roofed over in 1900, so it can no longer be seen. However, we do know something of the former healing rituals that were carried out here. Jones tells us that 'patients sat on a stone seat waiting for the 'troubling of the waters' as they called the periodic bubbles that suddenly arise from the bottom of the well: after which, they entered and bathed'.

## Ffynnon Fair *(121, 122)*

This is another well preserved monument and is located near the church (which replaced an earlier chapel called Tŷ Fair) in the village of Bryncroes. The well itself is certainly of some antiquity and the steps that lead down to it may have been added in the 17th century. The low wall that can be seen surrounding the well is of more recent date.

## Ffynnon Grasi *(123)*

A wire fence surrounds this well and it is now in a rather dilapidated state, though traces of the low boulder wall that surrounded it can be seen on one side of the large pool that forms this well. It is also interesting to note that the well is said to have been haunted by a woman called Grace (and still may be!), though how her ghost came to be associated with the well is unclear. There are a number of folk tales concerning ghosts and spirits at Welsh holy wells, and some of these may have ancient, pre-Christian roots, when a belief in well spirits seems likely. For example, at Ffynnon Gwenno in Carmarthenshire, the ghost of a woman called Gwenno is said to hover over the well on stormy nights when the moon is full.

## Felin Fach *(124)*

As Elfed Gruffydd mentions in his book, *Llŷn,* this small, but fine well was immortalised by the famous Welsh poet, Albert Evan Jones (also known as Cynan – his bardic name). He wrote longingly of the well 'Ffynnon Felin Fach' ('The Spring by the Little Mill') and other places in Llŷn, while he was fighting in France in the First World War. We can only imagine the powerful yearning that he must have had for the beauty of his native land, while facing the horrors of the trenches, but an extract from his poem gives us some idea.

O! let me taste again the joy
This spring could give me as a boy,
When water from some Heavenly Hill
With cleansing grace my heart would fill.

*(For a full inventory of the peninsula's former and current holy wells, see references for Gruffydd and Jones in the bibliography)*

# Bibliography

The literature on the prehistoric period in Britain and Europe is vast and a bibliography listing this would require a book in itself! Below however, I have listed some more general works that will provide a good starting point for any one wishing to know more about this hugely fascinating period. I have also listed some works that will be useful for further study of the Early Christian period. The titles marked with an * are highly recommended.

Alcock, L. 1960. Castell Odo: an embanked settlement on Mynydd Ystum, near Abedaron, Caernarvonshire. *Archaeologia Cambrensis* CIX-CX, 78–135 .

Basset, T.M & Davies, B.L. 1977. *Atlas of Caernarvonshire.* Gwynedd Rural Council.

Baring-Gould, S. & Burnard, R. 1904. An Exploration of some of the Cytiau in Tre'r Ceiri. *Archaeologia Cambrensis* IV, 1-17.

Berg, S. 1995. *The Landscape of the Monuments* (A study of the passage tombs in the Cúil Irra region, Co. Sligo, Ireland). Stockholm, Bureau for Archaeological Excavation.

Bowen, E.G. 1954. *The Settlements of the Celtic Saints in Wales.* Cardiff, Cardiff University Press.

Breese, C.E. 1932. Castell Odo. *Archaeologia Cambrensis* 1932, 372-386.

Ashe, G (ed.), 1971. *The Quest for Arthur's Britain.* London, Paladin.

*Bates, B. 2003. The Real Middle Earth: *Magic and Mystery in the Dark Ages.* London, Pan Books.

*Berresford Ellis, P. 2003. *A Brief History of The Celts.* London, Constable and Robinson, Ltd.

Brodie, N. 1994. *The Neolithic-Bronze Age Transition in Britain.* Oxford, British Archaeological Reports.

Budd, P. 2000. 'Meet the Metal Makers'. *British Archaeology* 56, 12-18.
*Burl, A. 1981. Rites of the Gods. London, J.M. Dent & Sons.

*Burl, A. 1989. *The Stonehenge People – Life and Death at the World's Greatest Stone Circle*. London, Barrie & Jenkins Ltd.

*Burl, A. 1997. *Prehistoric Astronomy and Ritual*. Princes Risborough, Shire Publications Ltd.

Chadwick, N. 1991. *The Celts*. London, Penguin.

Cobb, W.W, 1917. Note on the Cromlechs of Tan-y-Muriau. *Archaeologia Cambrenis*, 135-138.

Crew, P. 1985. The excavation of a group of mountain-top cairns on Drosgl, Llanllechid, Gwynedd. *Bulletin of the Board of Celtic Studies* 32, 309-314.

Cunliffe, B. 1978. *Iron Age Communities in Britain*. London, Routledge and Kegan Paul.

*Cunliffe, B (ed.), 1997. *Prehistoric Europe an Illustrated History*. Oxford, Oxford University Press.

*Cunliffe, B. 2001. *Facing the Ocean – the Atlantic and its peoples*. Oxford, Oxford University Press.

*Delaney, F. 1986. *The Celts*. London, BBC Publications/Hodder and Stoughton.

Dunn, C.J. 1976. *The Barrows of East Central Powys*. *Archaeologia Cambrensis* 126, 27-38.

*Dyer, J. 1992. *Hillforts of England and Wales*. Princes Risborough, Shire.

Dyer, J. 1990. *Ancient Britain*. London, B.T. Batsford.

Edmonds, M. 1995. *Stone Tools and Society – Working Stone in Neolithic and Bronze Age Britain*. London, B.T. Batsford Ltd.

Forde-Johnston, J. 1976. *Hillforts of the Iron Age in England and Wales*. Liverpool, Liverpool University Press.

*Garnham, T. 2004. *Lines on the Landscape Circles from the Sky – Monuments of Neolithic Orkney*. Stroud, Tempus.

Gibson, A. & Simpson, D (eds). *Prehistoric Ritual and Religion*. *Gloucestershire*, Sutton Publishing.

Griffiths, W.E. 1957. *The Typology and origins of Beakers in Wales*. Proceedings of the Prehistoric Society, 57-85.

*Gruffyd, E. 2003. *Llŷn*. Llanrwst, Gwasg Carreg Gwalch.

Jones, F. 1992. *The Holy Wells of Wales*. Cardiff, University of Wales Press.

Hadingham, E. 1983. *Early Man and the Cosmos*. London, William Heinemann Ltd.

Hogg, A.H.A. 1960. *Garn Boduan ad Tre'r Ceiri, Excavations at two Caernarvonshire Hill-Forts*. Archaeological Journal, 117, 1-38.

Hogg, A.H.A. 1975. *Hillforts of Britain*. London, Hart-Davis, Macgibbon.

Houlder, C. 1961. *The Excavation of a Neolithic Stone Implement Factory on Mynydd Rhiw in Caernarvonshire*. Proceedings of the Prehistoric Society, 108-143.

Hughes, H. 1907. *Report on the Excavations carried out at Tre'r Ceiri in 1906*. Archaeologia Cambrensis (VOL ?) 38-63.

James, S. & Rigby, V. 1997. *Britain and the Celtic Iron Age*. London. British Museum Press.

*Lynch, F. 1997. *Megalithic tombs and Long Barrows in Britain*. Princes Risborough, Shire Publications Ltd.

*Lynch, F., Aldhouse-Green, S. & Davies J.L. 2000. *Prehistoric Wales*. *Goucestershire*, Sutton Publishing.

Mackie, E. 1977. *The Megalith Builders*. London, Book Club Associates.

*Moffat, A. 2002. *The Sea Kingdoms – the History of Celtic Britain and Ireland*. London, HarperCollins.

Nash-Williams, V.E. 1950. *The Early Christian Monuments of Wales*. Cardiff, University of Wales Press.

O'Brien, P. 1996. *Bronze Age Copper Mining in Britain and Ireland.* Princes Risborough, Shire Publications Ltd.

Owen, E.A. 1890. *Holy Wells, or Water Veneration.* Archaeologia Cambrensis 1891, 8-17.

Parker Pearson, M. 1993. *Bronze Age Britain. London,* B.T. Batsford Ltd.

*Pitts, M. 2001. *Hengeworld.* London, Arrow Books.

Pollard, J. 1997. *Neolithic Britain.* Princes Risborough, Shire Publications Ltd.

Potter, T.W. & Johns, J. 1992. *Roman Britain.* London, British Museum Press.

Powell, T.G.E., Corcoran, J.X.W.P., Scott, J.G. & Lynch, F.M. 1969. *Megalithic Enquiries in the West of Britain.* Liverpool, Liverpool University Press.

*Pryor, F. 2003. *Britain BC – Life in Britain and Ireland before the Romans.* London, HarperCollins Publishers.

Raftery, B. 1994. *Pagan Celtic Ireland – The Enigma of the Irish Iron Age.* London, Thames and Hudson.

Raftery, J. (ed.). 1964 . *The Celts. Cork,* The Mercier Press.

Ralegh Radford, C.A. & Hemp, W.J. 1961. *Some Early Crosses in Caernarvonshire.* Transactions of the Caernarvonshire Historical society, 144-153

*Royal Commission on Ancient and Historical monuments in Wales and Monmouthshire.* 1960. Volume II: Central. London, Her Majesty's Stationery Office.

RCAHMW. 1964. Volume III: West. London, HMSO.

Senior, M. 1973. *Portrait of North Wales.* London, Robert Hale (now published by Gwasg Carreg Gwalch).

*Senior, M. 2003. *The Standing Stones of north-western Wales.* Llanrwst, Gwasg Carreg Gwalch.

*Senior M. 2005. *Hillforts of northern Wales*. Llanwrst, Gwasg Carreg Gwalch.

*Sharkey, J. 2004. *The Meeting of the Tracks: Rock Art in Ancient Wales*. Llanrwst, Gwasg Carreg Gwalch.

Taylor, J.J. 1994. *The First Golden Age of Europe was in Ireland and Britain* (circa 2400-1400 BC). *Ulster Journal of Archaeology* 57, 37-59.

Tilley, C. 1996. *The powers of rocks: topography and monument construction on Bodmin Moor.* World Archaeology 28, 161-176.

Turner, S. 2005. *Converting the British Landscape.* British Archaeology 84, 21-25.

Wadell, J. 2000. *The Prehistoric Archaeology of Ireland*. Co. Wicklow, Wordwell Ltd.

Williams, G. 1988. *The Standing Stones of Wales and South-West England*. British Archaeological Reports, British Series 197.

Whittle, A. 1996. *Europe in the Neolithic. The creation of new worlds. Cambridge*, Cambridge University Press.

# GAZETEER to Ancient Sites and Monuments in north-western Wales

Numbers in brackets are the grid references to the sites and monuments in the peninsula and can be used in conjunction with Ordnance Survey map Landranger 123 – Lleyn Peninsula, which covers our area of interest. Please remember that permission should be sought, when visiting sites and monuments on private land.

## *THE NEOLITHIC PERIOD (C. 4200-2500 BC)*

### NEOLITHIC TOMBS

**Bach Wen** (407495) *(1)*
This tomb is easily reached and lies just outside the village of Clynnog Fawr on the coast of Arfon. Follow the road down to Bach Wen Farm, and take the left turning. This leads you to a short footpath that takes you to the tomb. While you are here, it is also worth taking a look around inside the fine church which dates to the 14th century and you can also see the unusual sundial that stands in the church grounds (11th-early 12th century). If you head south for about half a mile from the church you will also see the holy well of Saint Beuno set back from the road on its left hand side (see below for grid reference)

**Cefn Isaf** (483408) *(2)*
Follow A497 towards Cricieth and take first left before the village of Llanystumdwy to the village of Rhos-lan. The tomb is situated in a field behind the village and can be reached by following a footpath, which is situated on the right, just before a row of houses. From here you can also visit the passage grave of Ystum Cegid Isaf if you wish and the standing stone at Betws Fawr is also not far away (see below).

### Ystum Cegid Isaf (498413) *(3)*

From above, walk east across fields down to the small bridge that crosses Afon Dwyfor. Walk across bridge, bear left and you will see a short farm track bordered by trees. Follow this to its end and then turn right and bear east for about half a mile. After climbing a low hill you will see a field wall heading east to a ridge of high land on the horizon. The passage grave is incorporated into this wall about half way along its length.

### Mynydd Cefnamwlch (230345) *(4)*

From the standing stone in St Peter's churchyard, Sarn Mellteyrn (see below for directions), keep going and follow minor road towards the B 4417. After about a mile and a half you will see the tomb on the lower slopes of Mynydd Cefnamwlch. A footpath provides easy access to the tomb.

### Tan y Muriau (237287) *(5) (6)*

Follow B 4413 towards the village of Botwnnog and follow the signs for Rhiw/Plas yn Rhiw (the main coastal road to Rhiw has been diverted because the cliff edge is very unstable just below Plas yn Rhiw country house (though at the time of writing, a new road is being built further up from the cliff). After skirting the lower slopes of Mynydd Rhiw you will drop down towards Plas yn Rhiw and just before the entrance into the estate, you will see a track on your left and a signpost for Tan y Muriau farmhouse. The long cairn is situated in a field, just behind the farmhouse.

The area around Rhiw is rich in ancient remains and you may also want to visit the ruined tomb at Bronheulog, Fynnon Aelrhiw holy well, Bryn Meillion hillfort, the standing stone at Capel Tan y Foel, the hillfort on Mynndd y Graig and the Neolithic axe factory and Early Bronze Age burial cairns on Mynydd Rhiw (see below for directions to these sites and monuments). The fine country house and beautiful gardens at Plas yn Rhiw are also worth a visit (house and gardens owned by National Trust so not open all year round).

### Y Ffôr (399384) (7)

Follow A499 north out of Pwllheli to the village of Y Ffôr. Just before the village you will see a farm track on the right, which leads down to Cromlech farm. Walk down this for a short way until you see farm buildings on your left and a field gate on your right. The tomb lies nearby in the field adjacent to the gate. Tir-Bach standing stone lies only about 1 mile from here (see below for directions).

### Mynydd Cilan (300235)

Follow road out of Abersoch towards Mynydd Cilan and keep going for about 2 miles until you see a silver National Trust sign for 'Muriau' on your left. Follow farm track to stile and follow path across fields (going through the left-hand gate) down to a secluded cove. Cross over small bridge and walk up sloping field to the metal gate at its top. Over this gate you will see the capstone of the ruined burial chamber lying in the adjacent field.

### Bronheulog (231281)

From Ffynnon Aelrhiw (for directions to well see 'Holy well' below) bear left across fields, heading in a south-easterly direction for about 350 yards and you will see the ruined tomb lying in a slightly sloping field.

### Penarth (430510)

Take minor road that leads inland from the village of Aberdesach, about a mile from Clynnog Fawr. About a quarter of a mile up this road you will come to a metal gate and just over this in the adjacent field you will see the small, collapsed tomb.

### Mynydd Rhiw Neolithic axe factory (234299)

From National Trust carpark at foot of Mynydd Rhiw follow footpath to summit of the headland until you come to the point where a small path leaves the main one. Just to the right of this small fork in the path you will see an expanse of gorse bordered by a stone wall. This is the location of the axe factory and you should be able to make out distinct hollows marking the Neolithic workings. If you plan to visit the site take some gloves and by searching among the gorse you should be able to find some of the waste material left behind by the Neolithic workforce. As mentioned previously, please do not remove any of this material from the site.

## EARLY BRONZE AGE (C. 2500-1500 BC)

## STANDING STONES

### St Peter's Churchyard (238327)
Take B 4413 to Sarn Mellteyrn. Turn left in village at Pen y Bont pub and then turn right up hill and then right again, taking the road that leads to the B 4417. You will find St Peter's churchyard a short way up this road and you will not miss the standing stone among the gravestones!

### Llangwnnadl (208325)
Follow B 4417 from Tudweiliog towards Llangwnnadl. The standing stone is located about 3 miles down this road in a field on the right and is clearly visible from the road.

### Pandy Saethon (287322)
Follow the B 4415 down the valley of the Afon Horon for about three-quarters of a mile and follow the steep farm track which is situated on the right just before the Inkermann Bridge. Walk up the track to the cottage and the standing stone is located nearby in a field in front of it.

### Nant y Gledrydd (293364)
Follow the B 4415 from the above and take the left turning near the farmhouse marked as 'Bodgadle' on the map. Follow road for about a mile and take the first right after 'Ty'n Lôn'. Follow the narrow wooded road for about a quarter of a mile and take first left. The standing stone is located in the field near the public footpath that leads to Morfa Nefyn.

### Yr Eifl (359436)

This standing stone can be seen on the way to Tre'r Ceiri and is located in a field on the right, about halfway along the lane that takes you to the footpath which leads to the hillfort (see below for directions).

### Tir Gwyn (344390/344392)

From the village of Llannor, take the road towards the house marked as 'Mela' on the map take the left turning just after this house and then first right, which takes you to Tir Gwyn farmhouse. The stones are located in a field to the right of the farmhouse

### Trallwyn (379417)

Take the B 4354 to the small village of Llwyndyrys and take first right at the phonebox in the village. Follow lane towards Penfras Uchaf farmhouse. Just before the farmhouse you will see a footpath on the right. Follow this until you come to the third gate on the left. Go through this and cross the field (keeping the field wall on your left) until you come to a gap in the left corner of the field. Go through this and turn right. You will see the standing stone in the corner of the field.

### Cefngraenog (455492)

Drive east for about a mile and half from Capel Uchaf and take the first left towards Graianog farmhouse. Follow this road for about a quarter of a mile until you come to a farmhouse on the right. The standing stone (and burial cairn) lies just a short way off in a field and can be reached by following the footpath that runs in front of the farmhouse.

### Glynllifon (445542)

To reach this standing stone simply go through the entrance which is located in the south-western corner of Glynllifon Country Park and you will see the monument standing in a field just in front of the gatehouse. You may also wish to visit the Bodfan standing stone from here (see below).

### Betws Fawr (464405)

From Llanystumdwy follow minor road towards Rhos-lan

and take second left near Tyddyn farm and then the first right at Betws Fawr. Follow the road for about a quarter of a mile until you see a farm track on your left. Walk along this to its end and you will see the standing stone in the middle of a field to the right of the track.

### Tyddyn Mawr (430444)
Follow lane down to Tyddyn Mawr farm until you come to farmyard. Go through the field gate to the left of the farmyard and bear left for a short distance through marshy ground towards a distinctive, flat-topped outcrop of rock. The standing stone is located in front of this.

### Tir-Bach (401401)
After passing through village of Y Ffôr, take first right and follow road for about half a mile until you come to Tir-Bach farm (first house on right). The standing stone is situated to the right of the farmhouse in marshy ground close to the river.

### Capel Tan y Foel (227277)
This standing stone can be reached by following the lane (first left) that leads off the road to Mynydd Penarfynydd. The stone is incorporated into the left-hand field wall a short way down the lane.

### Bodfan (442553)
From the Glynliffon stone follow road to Caernarfon and take first left. About half a mile down the road you will see a small post-box on the right, with a gate just before it on the left. Go through this gate and bear left for a short way across fields and you will see the stone.

### Llyn Glasfryn (405423/403424)
Take first right after Parc Glasfryn (where you see the sign for Ffynnon Gybi holy well) and follow road for about a quarter of a mile until you come to the entrance to the Glasfryn estate on the left (you will see a gate with stone globes and a gatehouse). Walk up drive to the mansion and go through the first gate on your right, which leads to Llyn

Glasfryn. Walk through the fields around the edge of the lake until you come to its eastern end and you will clearly see the larger of the standing stones on a low hill (because of its height you will see the standing stone sometime before you reach it). To reach the smaller standing stone from the larger one, simply go through the gate in the corner of the field and then through the gap in the field wall. Ffynnon Grasi holy well lies almost immediately behind the larger of the Glasfryn stones.

### Gyrn Ddu (396462)
From the village of Llanaelhaearn take the first right in front of the Rivals pub. Follow for about a mile and take the lane, which leads towards Penllechog farm. Take the first right before Penllechog and you will come to a stile just in front of another farmhouse with outbuildings. Cross the stile and follow the footpath until you come to a ruined farm building. Take a right past this, turn left and continue following footpath until you see the derelict farmhouse, where the standing stone can be seen incorporated into the wall in front of it. The burial cairns on Gyrn Ddu can be 'easily reached' from here (reaching them does involve a strenuous climb) and you may also wish to carry on to the cairn on the summit on Bwlch Mawr (see below).

### Plas ym Mhenllech (220344)
From Mynydd Cefnamwlch tomb follow road down to B 4417. Drive south, take first right at Penllech and follow lane down to Plas ym Mhenllech farm. The stone can be seen standing at the end of the wall of St Mary's Church (which you may want to look round), where it forms part of the entrance into a yard at the farm.

### Morfa Abererch (420355)
Cross level crossing at Morfa Abererch and follow footpath which leads to the beach. Walk along the beach and head east for a short distance, until you see a low promontory. You will see the standing stone on top of this, partially buried in the sand dune.

### Glan Afon (393360)

From Pwllheli, follow the A497 towards Cricieth. The standing stone is located about 1 mile outside the town, in a field on the right-hand side of the road, in front of the house is marked as 'Glan Afon' on the map

## BURIAL CAIRNS

### Mynydd Carnguwch (374429)

From Llithfaen, follow the road to Llanaelhaearn for about a mile and take the path that leads past the farm buildings marked 'Hafod' on the map. This path runs around the bottom of Mynydd Carnguwch and from here, you can reach the cairn on the summit. However, a word of warning – although the cairn is hugely impressive, it is a steep climb to the top of Mynydd Carnguwch!

### Tre'r Ceiri (374447)

This much ruined cairn can be seen when visiting the hillfort at Tre'r Ceiri and is situated on the highest point of the site (see below).

### Yr Eifl (365448)

The best way to reach the two cairns on the western peak of the mountain, is by following the path which leads from the foot of Tre'r Ceiri to its summit. Again, it should be pointed out that this is also not an easy climb, though it is one that is well worth the effort.

### Gyrn Ddu eastern summit (406467)

From the Gyrn Ddu standing stone, walk around to the back of the derelict farmhouse and you will find a public footpath, which takes you through the uplands to the pass below Bwlch Mawr. Follow this footpath over two stiles and after the second stile, to your right you will see the remains of a prehistoric farm (possibly Iron Age), which is well worth a look. After this carry on for a short way until you see a 19th century field wall on your left, climbing up the eastern summit of Gyrn Ddu. The cairns can be reached by following this field wall, which passes through the two cairns. Again, this is a strenuous climb, but as with the other cairns that are hard to reach, there are superlative views from these two monuments.

### Western summit (396466)

I could not wholeheartedly recommend that people visit this cairn, as it is not particularly impressive and not easy to reach. However, if you wish to do so, head west from the above to the striking rock formation which marks the western summit. The cairn is located at the southern end of the summit and can be reached by climbing up its tumbled slopes, though be careful when doing so (do not climb summit when it is wet).

It is also worth mentioning here that the remains of a prehistoric settlement can be seen about 450 yards to the north-west of the western summit and you may wish to visit this. To reach the settlement, walk to the summit's northern end and cross the wall that you will see. Walk downhill for a short way and you will not only find the settlement, but will also be rewarded with a breathtaking view.

### Bwlch Mawr (425477)

From the probable Iron Age farm near Gyrn Ddu eastern summit, continue walking along the footpath for about a mile and a half until you come to a stile below the summit of Bwlch Mawr. Cross this and skirting the boulder field head north to the summit of the mountain and you will find the cairn not far from an Ordnance Survey triangulation point.

### Foel Gron (300313)

From the car park at the foot of Foel Gron, follow the path which leads to its summit and you will easily see the cairn.

### Cefngraeanog (455491)

This small, kerbed cairn lies just in front of the Cefngraeanog standing stone (see above).

## Mynydd Rhiw cairns (232294, 232296)

From the site of the axe factory keep following the path to the summit of the headland and you will find the cairns spread along the ridge below the summit (you will see the largest cairn as you approach it from a distance).

## Garn Fadrun (280351)

This cairn can be found by climbing the summit above the cluster of huts that are located on the western side of the hillfort's interior.

# THE IRON AGE (C. 750-43 AD)

## HILLFORTS

### Tre'r Ceiri (373446)

To reach Tre'r Ceiri take the first left from the crossroads in Llithfaen (as you are heading towards Llanaelhaearn on the B 4417) and follow the lane to its end. Here, you will find a footpath that is easily followed to the hillfort.

### Garn Boduan (312393)

Head towards Morfa Nefyn on the A 497. After passing through Boduan, take the first right and continue along for a short way until you see a small carpark and gate on the left. From here follow the footpath that leads through the forestry commission plantation to the hillfort (take the left path where the footpath splits in two)

### Garn Fadrun (280352)

In the centre of Garn Fadrun village you will find a footpath just before the church on the right. This will take you to the hillfort.

### Craig y Ddinas (448520)

From Glynliffon country park follow A 499 towards Pontllyfni and take first left and keep following road and go left again as the road climbs above the valley of the Afon Llyfni (You may also want to take a look at Pont y Cim, which is a fine 17th century packhorse bridge that crosses the river nearby). After a short while you will come out above the valley and the road will level out. On your right, you will see a gate and in the adjacent field you will plainly see the tops of the ramparts of the fort a short distance away.

### Carn Pentyrch (424417)
From the western side of Llangybi holy well, follow the footpath, which leads around the edge of the wood that climbs behind the well. Keep following path through the wood and go through gap in the wall that runs across the top. Walk up the hill, go through another gap in a field wall and follow path to fort.

### Castell Odo (187284)
Follow the B 4413 to Aberdaron. The hillfort lies about two miles outside the village and you will see the low slopes of Mynydd Ystum on your right as you approach Aberdaron. To reach the fort, go through the gate near the large stone barn at the foot of the hill and walk up farm track to the stile. Cross stile and bear right, following path to the hillfort.

### Bryn Meillion (230283)
This small fort lies just outside Rhiw and is situated just behind the house that shares its name with the fort.

### Mynydd y Graig (228274)
From Capel Tan y Foel, walk down road into Rhiw and take footpath on first right that leads past cottages to a gate. Go right through gate and follow footpath up Mynydd y Graig to stile. Climb over stile and follow path left up onto the summit, where you will see the remains of the hillfort.

### Dinas Dinlle (437563)
Turn off A 499 and follow road down to Dinas Dinlle. There is a footpath to the fort near the playground in the middle of the village.

### Pen y Gaer (428455)

Take first right before the Rivals pub in Llanaelhaearn and follow road up past Cwm Coryn Farm and take left-hand footpath just after the 'homestead'. Follow this for about a mile until it begins to drop down, bear left up valley towards western slopes of Pen y Gaer and you will find an ancient track leading up to the hillfort. An ancient settlement can also be seen in this vicinity, though not much remains of it today.

### Porth Dinllaen (275417)

Hardly anything remains of this promontory fort today, though dedicated hillfort enthusiasts can follow the road that runs across Nefyn golf course and where it begins to descend to the picturesque fishing village at Porth Dinllaen, you will see a short stretch of bank and ditch on your left.

### Pared Mawr (304247)

Follow the road out of Abersoch for about 2 miles. Just after you have passed the church and phonebox on your right, looking left you will catch sight of the rampart that surrounds the fort. The best way of approaching the fort is from the fields that lie opposite the farmhouse just up the road from the church.

## THE EARLY CHRISTIAN PERIOD
## (C. 450-850 AD)

## EARLY CHRISTIAN STONES

### St Hywyn's (173263)

Inside St Hywyn's church in Aberdaron. The stones can be visited when the church is open or by prior arrangement with the Rev. Evelyn Davies (see website address below).

### Llanaelhaearn (387448)

The Melitus stone can be seen in the graveyard underneath the yew trees near the gate, while the other probable

Christian Stone can be seen in the low wall that surrounds the church. Just behind this you will see the unmarked rough stone slab, which may also be an Early Christian stone. The other inscribed stone is built into the west wall of the transept inside the church.

### Llangian (295290)

Enter churchyard and follow path around to the right of church. You will see the stone standing on the grass, near a fine gravestone.

### Llannor (353373)

This monument is located just inside the doorway to Llannor church, although unfortunately, the church is often closed. However, arrangements can be made to view the stone (contact: Rev. Andrew Jones, Ty'n Llan, Lanbedrog, Pwllheli, Gwynedd)

### Plas Glyn y Weddw (329315)

These stones can be seen inside the entrance porch of the impressive Plas Glyn y Weddw country house, which is located in the village of Llanbedrog close to the beach. It is well worth taking a look around the house itself, as it contains interesting artefacts relating to the its history and a number of rooms are given over to the display of some fine paintings by artists from the locality and from further afield in Wales.

### Cefn Coch (422408)

On the right-hand gatepost of the lane leading to Cefn Coch, which is one of a number of houses that lie about half a mile south-west of Llangybi church and can be found just past the school. Although the cross is now faint, it can still be seen on closer inspection of the stone.

### Llangybi (429412)

Situated just inside gateway into churchyard, on the left.

### Capel Uchaf (430498)

To find this stone take the minor road that leads to Upper

Clynnog (head for Capel Uchaf). After about a mile you will come to a row of council houses on your right. The stone is incorporated into the low wall that lies just past these on the left, where the road begins to turn.

**Bryncir** (482455)
This bilingual Christian stone, which features a Latin and Ogam inscription is located in Llystyn Gwyn farmyard, which lies just off the A 487 between Caernarfon and Porthmadog.

**Pistyll** (319418)
This monument is located about half a mile to the west of Pistyll church and is located in wall opposite the lay-by on the road leading down to Nefyn.

**Clynnog Fawr** (414497)
This ancient sundial can be seen in the churchyard at Clynnog Fawr, close to the church tower.

## HOLY WELLS

**Ffynnon Gybi** (427412)
Take A 499 from Pwllheli and after about 4 miles you will see the signpost for the well at the first right after Parc Glasfryn. Follow road to Llangybi and just before the village you will see a footpath sign for the well on the left. Follow footpath across fields and down the track which brings you to the well.

**Ffynnon Aelrhiw** (233284)
From Plas yn Rhiw country house (or Tan y Muriau) follow the narrow lane that leads towards Mynydd Rhiw. After a short way you will see a footpath sign on your left. Cross stile and follow footpath south-west across fields for about 200 yards and you will see the remains of the holy well surrounded by a clump of trees and bushes.

### Ffynnon Fair (226313)
This holy well is situated just off the road near the church in the village of Bryncroes.

### Ffynnon Aelhaearn (384446)
Situated just around the corner from Llanaelhaearn church, just off the B 4417 on the left-hand side of the road.

### Ffynnon Beuno (413494)
From Clynnog Fawr, follow road for about 200 yards south and you will see the well set back on the left.

### Ffynnon Felin Fach (365354)
This well is easily reached by simply following the A497 from Pwllheli and taking first right near Pensarn Farm. The well lies about half a mile along the road on the right, opposite a house of the same name.

### Ffynnon Fyw (309308)
Follow minor from Abersoch through the beautiful village of Llangian and take right for Mynytho at Coed-y-fron farm. Take third right down this road and you will soon see the late 19th century Horeb chapel. Follow the footpath, which runs alongside the chapel and after a short way you will see this fine well.

### Ffynnon Grasi (404423)
To reach this well, simply walk a couple of hundred yards east from the larger of the two standing stones at Llyn Glasfryn and you will see the ruined well surrounded by wire fencing.

### Ffynnon Saint (242294)
Follow coastal road above Porth Neigwl and follow footpath through the forestry plantation on lower slopes of Mynydd Rhiw. Follow footpath past Ty'n y Parc, walk through forest and take path as it turns left and climbs uphill. At the top of the path you will see some stone steps. These will lead you to the well.

## USEFUL WEB-SITES AND ADDRESSES

www.st-hywyn.org.uk – information on the Veracius and Senacus stones and the history of St Hywyn's church in Aberdaron.

Royal Commission on the Ancient & Historical Monuments of Wales – Plas Crug, Aberystwyth, Ceridigion, SY23 1NJ.

NMR. Wales@rcahmw.org.uk – the RCAHMW web-site also includes the excellent Coflein mapping service, which allows you to look at the huge number of sites and monuments in the peninsula and those elsewhere in Wales (there are also some superb aerial photographs of some of the peninsula's hillforts).

Gwynedd Archaeological Trust – Craig Beuno, Ffordd y Garth, Bangor, Gwynedd LL57 2RT.
www.heneb.co.uk

Gwynedd Art Museum and Gallery.